W ith the establishment of the Republic of the United States of America, a great landmark in secular history was erected: it was the first time a nation was ever founded on reasoned political principles, proceeding from the axiom that man's birthright is freedom. And as long as those principles were maintained, it succeeded beyond all precedent. Whoever is fortunate enough to be an American citizen came into the greatest inheritance man has ever enjoyed. He has had the benefit of every heroic and intellectual effort men have made for many thousands of years, realized at last. If Americans should now turn back, submit again to slavery, it would be a betrayal so base the human race might better perish.

Isabel Paterson, 1943

———❈———

This book is dedicated to those for whom
America's Declaration of Independence
and original Constitution mean
what The Founders intended.

The Unfounding of America

A COUNTDOWN TO TOO LATE

Michael Russell

Éditions Nonesmanneslond

By Michael Russell

The Unfounding of America

Winterdanse: The Misplaced Art of Snow Ballet

Once Upon a Time on a Bicycle

Honor Student

Forthcoming

Little Girl, Big Lie

Knights of the Eleventh Hour

The Inquisition of Don Miguel

COUNTING DOWN

  • The Pitiful Push
  • Staying a Wrongful Course While Knowing the Truth
  • The Inevitable Emptiness of Teenage Activism
  • Justice Gone Awry at the Ballot Box
  • Closing One Eye While Believing with the Other
  • The Answer to Leftist News
  • Breathing Life into Mistakes of the Past
  • No Business Like Show Business
  • Investing in The Label Factory
  • The Pious-Pundit Pulpit
  • Easy Street
  • Facebook Fools and YouTube Yellowbellies
  • Acquiescing to the Essentially Anti-American
  • A Gentleman's Wager

Who? Or True?

I first came to understand what America had been founded to enshrine and protect when on a solo bicycling expedition from California to New Hampshire in the summer of 1982. Two years later, while observing audience response to a debate between calmly articulate *laissez-faire* capitalists and rabidly emotional Democratic Socialists, I saw America's likely fate and knew that the hope for an American future was educational, not political.

It was obvious that by producing citizens progressively less and less able to think conceptually, America's system of public education was achieving a post-America future, which inspired me in 1989 to write the novel *Honor Student*. But I did not realize until twenty years later that the finalizing component of this contrivance was *perceptual*, that government-controlled corporate media was prescribing what trusting Americans, habituated to ingesting spoon-fed information, perceived.

This was and remains a masterful endeavor: strip developing minds of the ability to *reason* about reality while depriving all minds of the ability to *see* reality. By 2020, the clash I witnessed in that opposing-systems debate had become a brazen celebration of public education's true goal: the creation of a citizenry incapable of thinking independently.

When in 2023 I posted a series of video essays as a draft for this book, I challenged a dangerous assumption made plain during the Covid ruse. I asked: "How much information, news, and advice do you accept as true because of the messenger's credentials or title? How much of what you accept do you personally know to be true? To what extent are you willing to surrender 'I know' for 'they say'? What if your health, happiness, liberty, and life depend upon your answers to these questions?"

Uniforms, badges, degrees, familial status, bestseller-list rank, celebrity, and government titles are irrelevant when applied to news and advice, rules and regulations, directives, edicts, prohibitions, permissions, orders, and law because what matters is not *who*, but *true*.

Droite? Or Gauche?

Whether or not America's first "Republicans" organized in good faith to prevent their constitutional republic from being "democratically" supplanted, the subsequent two-party artifice has since produced an illusion of choice between resolute paths to an anti-America destination. Historically, Republicans proposed material autonomy with government dominion over consciousness and morality; Democrats advocated spiritual choice with control over action and production. Both appropriated each other's lingo and policy according to political expediency, and both unapologetically agreed that the proper function of government is not protector of inalienable rights, but parent of irresponsible dependents. The details over which party loyalists publicly bickered were and remain a peripheral distraction from a larger goal.

Republican versus Democrat, Conservative versus Progressive, Right versus Left are little-picture constructs designed to perpetuate big-picture political and moral larceny. In elections of significance, citizens are encouraged to credit Candidates A and B as "the people's choice" when both are strained through filters designed to cultivate *this* particular Candidate A and *that* particular Candidate B. Regardless of either's little-picture vows, both will in the big picture play for the anti-liberty side or not be permitted to play.

This opposing-wings deception, from its French National Assembly seating-arrangement origin through every ensuant obfuscatory redefining, becomes obvious at its non-oppositional extremes where force waits as a closing argument. Only wannabe masters and serfs praise a system where citizens are expected to choose between compulsion on one side, compulsion on the other, and eternal compromise juggling in a make-believe "moderate" middle. And yet, the Right-Left-spectrum lie has for more than two centuries been reversing the unprecedented achievement that was America.

By contrast, the human-liberty spectrum is authentic. It is

the sole ethics-derived plane of demarcation. At one end, free humans stand upright. At the other, slaves grovel and suffer. Between legitimate extremes of dignity preserved and dignity surrendered exists an admixture of standards, hopes, and goals; of want for independence, orders, rescue. Prior to the birth of the nation of America, social systems worldwide accepted the supposition that masters and serfs are a fact of life and, like charity given only to be withdrawn, human liberty vacillated according to government caprice and citizen assent.

But the Republic of America was founded on reasoned political principles proceeding from the axiom that man's birthright is freedom, and because America's founding documents championed an inviolable defense of that axiom on behalf of the lone political system in history created to preserve human liberty, Republicans of the 1850s needed no self-descriptor other than — or higher than — *American*. Which means, since Democracy is a mob-rule-by-vote version of the master-and-serf society, when Americans accepted the two-party paradigm they legitimized mob rule and enabled a divide-to-control ploy disguised as "choice." There is no human-liberty-spectrum difference between a monarch trumpeting Royal Decrees, a dictator issuing orders, a majority issuing orders, and political syndicates hawking compromise. All are anti-liberty and contrary to the principles that inspired authorship of America's founding documents.

Although "Leftist" is ascribed in the following pages to proponents of socialism and communism, such use does not imply that "Rightists" do not similarly regard life and production as property of The State. In the political picture, Right and Left are aligned against liberty and *not* opposites on any meaningful spectrum. They are a two-door trap baited with artificially flavored enticements. In the human picture, the only opposites on the only spectrum of import are liberty and enslavement.

Bargains between the two will always serve enslavement.

Michael Russell
May 2024/May 2025

REQUIEM

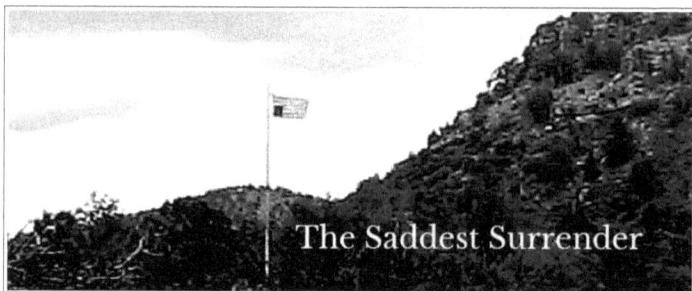

The Saddest Surrender

Her wagon ruts are mapped and paved
From sea to shining sea,
Her homesteads cloned, approved, and cubed,
Our home of the brave,
Once land of the free.

What for granted we took before dewy-eyed sleep
We awaken to see by dawn's early light:
Not broad stripes and bright stars,
Not America proud,
But a nation renounced and a sad flag blanched white.

With, "When in the course of human events"
Bold men wrote Liberty's doctrine,
They shattered the chains of monarch and master,
Naming and claiming
The citizen sovereign.

But steadily, steadily, downward so steadily,
Nudged from a summit courageously earned,
Blindly, blindly, shamefully blindly,
Americans played
While America burned.

Jefferson, Adams, Hancock, and Lee
Pledged what few know today to be real,
With fifty-two peers they bound
Life, wealth, and honor
In Liberty's name for a nation ideal.

"Shirtsleeves to shirtsleeves
In three generations"
Is a saw ever-tragically prescient,
In commerce, in art, in the building of nations,
Resolute Man becomes cowed Acquiescent.

But sadder still and saddest most
In our We the People endeavor?
Without rocket's red glare or bombs bursting in air
We, the People, re-delivered to chains
Our children and theirs, most likely forever.

Was it fingers-crossed hope? Second-hand trust?
The fear of a life self-reliant?
What kept us from seeing?
Kept our eyes and minds closed?
Made us docile and passive, afraid and compliant?

Following, following, like drunkards all swallowing
The promise of safety, convenience, and ease,
We sold for a dime our autonomous souls
To creators of nothing, to takers of all,
To parasites, leeches, cockroaches, fleas.

So much for so little was tossed to the wind,
Traded for trinkets, for debt ocean-deep,
Though forewarned and forearmed
Through our fingers it passed:
The Republic we failed, were unable to keep.

What spark may remain remains smothered beneath
The dependents on whom their masters relied,
But the answer to "shirtsleeves" is a saw for the strong,
With the will to relearn
And past lessons applied . . .

What one man has done may another in turn.

THE UNFOUNDING OF AMERICA:
A Countdown to Too Late

AMERICA AND THE LAW OF IDENTITY

The collectivist Left's war on words, on the terms used to describe and communicate reality-based concepts, should by now be obvious to anyone who esteems reality as unalterable by wish, whim, or political decree. The Left's journey into double-speak has advanced to the fore like a fashion craze or pop-music hit or novel virus with flu-like symptoms. Orwell's "blackwhite" is suddenly everywhere as a raucous public phenomenon accompanied by a malevolent belligerence intended to silence anyone who questions its legitimacy or, sin of sins, who sees and names its purpose.

Education is not indoctrination, freedom of speech is not conditional, rights and privileges are not interchangeable, health care is not coercive, justice is not subjective, gender is not re-assignable, journalism is not the parroting of party doctrine, news is not agenda-driven fiction or selective omission, violent riots are not peaceful protests, the peaceful assertion of parental judgment is not terrorism, science is not consensus, facts are not amenable to majority vote, truth is not obedient to wish, whim, or political decree. Reality is not, as lapel buttons once sported by

Washington politicians proclaimed, negotiable. Education, free speech, censorship, choice, rule of law, liberty, rights, justice, terrorism, biological distinction, tyranny, and all the rest are as concepts singularly objectively definable.

One word in particular, however, is not among those openly culled for redesignation. It is a word that represents an idea collectivists and authoritarians have been attempting to destroy for as long as that idea has existed — a word conversationally employed to evoke a conditioned emotional response while remaining specifically undefined — a word whose true meaning is intended not merely to be changed, but eradicated. Where politics are concerned, it could even be called The Original.

The word is *America* and, by extension, *Americans*.

Question: Do mountains, rivers, lakes, coastlines, and amber waves of grain make America, *America*? What about her climate, culture, flag, national anthem, industry, military, politicians, citizenry, cities, and patriotic pride?

No. Like trim on a building or clothing on a person, these are but attributes peripheral to foundation, framework, soul. What makes America *America* is her Declaration of Independence and Constitution.*

With unprecedented wisdom and vision, America was founded to endure as an entity unique in all the world. Should she cease to be *that* entity, that Constitutional Republic derived from a Declaration of Independence, she will cease to be America.

Which is why there is no such thing as an American Communist, an American Fascist, an American Socialist, an American Nazi, or an American Leftist. And although there are innumerable Marxists *in* America, there is no such thing as American Marxism. There is America, and there is *not* America; Americans, and *not* Americans.

The concept is as clean as the Law of Identity. Just as

A can only be A, America can only be America. Just as the
same attribute cannot at the same time belong and not belong to the same subject in the same respect, an un- or
anti-Constitutional "America" is not America. When what
defines America no longer exists, when the principles that
gave birth to the idea and manifestation of America no
longer exist — whether as a result of innocent error, incremental betrayal, or overnight putsch — the *thing* that takes
its place will not be America.

Those who defame America's defining principles are
not Americans. They are the unhealthy inhabitants of a
nation created to be healthy, weaklings unwilling to rise to
the standard of a free independent citizenry seeking instead to subvert that standard by nullifying the definition
of standard and even the definition of definition.

America's defining principles are not an inspiration
for faux Americans, but reminders of personal impotence.
Their life-view requires not that they become more, but
that they make America less. Their response to what
makes America, America, is not to honor her virtues but to
invert them in service of their desire to be rulers and minions, distributors and recipients of the unearned, ship-
wreck survivors voting on who next to eat for dinner.

They don't want to *pursue* happiness, they want it as a
gift. They don't want to *achieve* liberty; achievement is an
imposition and liberty is too much trouble to maintain.
They reject the right to free speech because an open ex-
change of ideas threatens *their* propaganda. They reject
the right to bear arms because an armed citizenry can defend itself against *them*.

In short, *they don't want to be American*. It's too hard. It
demands too much independence, integrity, responsibility, self-esteem — too much Americanism. They want A to
be non-A while evading the burden of calling the non-A

by a new name. Their want to play musical chairs with reality in the hope that *someone other than them* will be left without a chair when the music stops. When they look in the mirror, no matter what they tell themselves they see, theirs is not an American reflection.

That is the simple truth. This is how true Americans, *Constitution-honoring Americans*, can use it.

At the outset of every discussion about politics, true Americans must establish what their nation is and is not. Whether that discussion opens with "Did you vote for so-and-so?" or "Do you think national borders are necessary?" or "Are you opposed to a federal minimum wage?" a primary question must be asked and the answer mutually understood before conversation can meaningfully proceed.

That question is: What is the definition of America?

Not "What does America mean to you?" or "What do you think America means to Republicans or Democrats or the rest of the world?" But strictly and purely, "What is the definition of America?"

If the answer is not what America was founded to be — a constitutional republic derived from a declaration of the inalienable rights of men — and the respondent cannot be helped to appreciate the Law of Identity, true Americans are morally entitled to decline further discussion and to recommend citizenship in any nation by definition not America.

Which is, of course, a recommendation that applies unprejudicially to every species of faux American regardless of political-party affiliation.

While "Leftist" references proponents of socialism and communism, the label does not imply that "Rightists" do not similarly regard life and production as property of The State. Where inalienable rights are concerned, there is no difference between a Constitution-betraying Democrat and a Constitution-betraying Republican, and for most of America's history Democrats and Republicans have competed to replace the uniquely American definition of government as *protector of inalienable rights* with *parent of irresponsible dependents*. Only wannabe masters offer as "options" compulsion in one hand and compulsion in the other. Only wannabe serfs accept such a liberty-defiling non-choice. Only shortsighted history-dismissing pragmatists believe that compromise juggling around a make-believe "middle" will lead to anything other than a history-repeated master-and-serf society.

The more overtly faux Americans betray America's defining principles, the more they are cornered into accusing true Americans of advocating their own treasonous thoughts, words, and deeds. Such projection is the metier of deceivers. Had these con artists a scintilla of integrity they would acknowledge that remaking America into anything other than America requires canceling America and choosing for their goal a new name.

"AImerica," "The Technate," "Trumpublica,""USA 2.0," "Palantir, Inc.," "The Nation Formerly Known as America," "Greater Israel West," and "X" are, as of this writing, applicable and available. "Oceana" compliments AI plagiarism. "Obamaland," "Clintonia," "Bidenburg," and "Antifaschtan" have for the moment faded from fashion but, like all merchandisable trends, may return. The Left can choose by a show of hands; the Right by Executive Order.

Until that day, no pretense will ever alter the fact that *America is her Declaration and Constitution* and that she cannot at the same time be anything else.

---

* See Chapter Two for a list of Declaration- and Constitution-contradicting post-Bill of Rights amendments.

TAKING JUSTICE BACK
FROM DEAD HANDS: A PREMISE

In 1937, Napoleon Hill wrote: "When men first come into contact with crime they abhor it. If they remain in contact with crime they become accustomed to it and endure it. If they remain in contact long enough they embrace it and become influenced by it."[1]

Not since America was a frontier has crime been so overtly and routinely, even casually, committed against her citizens. Not since American frontier towns had to send word to a U.S. marshal two or three days distant has justice been so conspicuously absent. Not since organized crime ruled America's city streets — with judges, politicians, and lawmen in pocket — has the corruption of justice been so prevalent.

America is today vacillating between the stages of enduring and embracing criminality. There can be no doubt that her culture has become, perhaps irreversibly, influenced by it.

Rampant theft in retail stores — not sneaky shoplifting, but open mob-orchestrated robbery without fear of apprehension or repercussion — is a fact of life, a new normal. A growing number of major retailers have abandoned a growing number of cities due to unsafe conditions for business, employees, and customers. Business owners have reasonably threatened to stop paying property tax until authorities put an end to crime. A television reporter employed by a network in denial of government-policy-induced criminal violence was the victim of a smash-and-grab theft while reporting on thriving lawlessness. Throughout the 2020 Summer of Thuggery, property, businesses, and lives were destroyed, largely without legal consequence. During Lori Lightfoot's single term as mayor of Chicago, the city logged 2300 homicides and 9000 shootings.

Bodyguard-protected Leftist politicians cry "Defund the police!" and then express surprise when their homes get painted with Black Lives Matter and Antifa graffiti. Catch-and-release is no longer a term used by sport fishermen, but the modus operandi of George Soros-funded district attorneys across America,[2] not to mention all along America's southern border. Under New York City's bail-reform law, suspects with criminal histories released without bail are re-arrested at a rate of sixty-plus percent, ninety-plus percent of which are for felony and violent crimes. A Manhattan policeman, commenting on forced overtime and days-off work mandates, estimated that 1400 officers will resign by the end of 2023 *before* qualifying for retirement, even more, he said, than 2022's record of 1297 early exits.

The Oregon Retail-Crime Association reported that Portland stores lose $5 million a year to theft. Nike asked officials in that city for permission to post off-duty police officers with the power to arrest shoplifters. Philadelphia has experienced its worst violent-crime surge in three centuries of history. An apartment-management company in Austin, Texas, citing "security concerns," announced that its residents would not be allowed to leave or enter their homes between the hours of 10:00 pm and 5:00 am. And with property crime in Milwaukee up twenty-six percent since 2020, in response to a Wisconsin-senate-floor discussion about crime spreading to Milwaukee suburbs, Senator LaTonya Jackson exclaimed, "Fuck the suburbs . . . they don't know a goddamn thing about how life is in the city."

While violent- and property-crime statistics continue to climb across America, America's traitorous attorney general wants to ban the FBI from using these statistics to guide or inform law enforcement — not that the FBI can be trusted to publish anything unmanipulated or un-redacted. The American judicial system's widespread failure to honor Americans' constitutionally guaranteed right to a speedy and public trial, combined with its explicit willingness to prosecute for political gain and with naked partiality, is now embraced as a weapon by the legally powerful and endured by the legally powerless who, to avail themselves of effective representation, are drained of everything they have earned while living virtuous lives.

Unless the only place *you* get your news is from sources that filter and omit the facts that contradict the regime's "everything's fine" narrative, you already know this. If your eyes and ears are open to non-agenda-influenced voices and if your mind still functions independently, you already have the picture and you have probably asked the lamentable question:

What are Americans to do when America's justice system
fails to uphold the laws written to protect them?

ONE HUNDRED AND TWENTY-TWO years ago, in his novel, *The Virginian*, Owen Wister provided a true and timeless answer. In that prodigious chronicle, a Vermont school teacher new to the Wyoming frontier learns that the man she loves participated in the lynching of a cattle thief, a thief whom the law had for years allowed to deprive honest citizens of their property. When the couple who brought the teacher west from New England witness the woman's confusion and despair, they ask their neighbor, a retired judge, to help in her grief.[3]

> Judge Henry sat thinking, waiting until school should be out. He did not at all relish what lay before him. He would like to have got out of it. He had been a federal judge; he had been an upright judge; he had met the responsibilities of his difficult office not only with learning, which is desirable, but also with courage and common sense besides, and these are essential. He had been a staunch servant of the law. And now he was invited to defend that which, at first sight, nay even at second and third sight, must always seem a defiance of the law . . .
>
> "I sent him myself on that business," the Judge reflected uncomfortably. "I am partly responsible for the lynching. It has brought him one great unhappiness already through the death of Steve. If it gets running in this girl's mind, she may — dear me!" the judge broke off, "what a nuisance!" And he sighed. For as all men know, he also knew that many things should be done in this world in silence, and that talking about them is a mistake.

But when school was out, and the girl gone to her cabin, his mind had set the subject in order thoroughly, and he knocked at her door, ready, as he had put it, to sacrifice his character in the cause of true love.

"Well," he said, coming straight to the point, "some dark things have happened." And when she made no answer to this, he continued: "But you must not misunderstand us. We're too fond of you for that."

"Judge Henry," said Molly Wood, also coming straight to the point, "have you come to tell me that you think well of lynching?"

He met her. "Of burning Southern negroes in public, no. Of hanging Wyoming cattle thieves in private, yes. You perceive there's a difference, don't you?"

"Not in principle," said the girl, dry and short.

"Well," said the Judge, easy and thoughtful, "what do you mean by principle?"

"I didn't think you'd quibble," flashed Molly. "I'm not a lawyer myself." . . .

"I don't mean to quibble," he assured her. "I know the trick of escaping from one question by asking another. But I don't want to escape from anything you hold me to answer. If you can show me that I am wrong, I want you to do so. But," and here the Judge smiled, "I want you to play fair, too."

"And how am I not?"

"I want you to be just as willing to be put right by me as I am to be put right by you. And so when you use such a word as principle, you must help me to answer by saying what principle you mean. For in all sincerity I see no likeness in principle whatever between burning Southern negroes in public and hanging Wyoming horse thieves in private. I consider the burning a proof that the South is semi-barbarous, and the hanging a proof that Wyoming is determined to become civilized. We do not torture our criminals. We do not invite spectators to enjoy their death agony. We put no such hideous disgrace upon the United States. We execute our criminals by the swiftest means, and in the quietest way. Do you think the principle is the same?"

Molly had listened to him with attention. "The way is different," she admitted.

"Only the way?"

"Both defy law and order."

"Ah, but do they both? Now we're getting near the principle."

"Why, yes. Ordinary citizens take the law in their own hands."

"The principle at last!" exclaimed the Judge. "Now tell me: Out of whose hands do they take the law?"

"The court's."

"What made the courts?"

"I don't understand."

"How did there come to be any courts?"

"The Constitution."

"How did there come to be any Constitution? Who made it?"

"The delegates, I suppose."

"Who made the delegates?"

"I suppose they were elected, or appointed, or something."

"And who elected them?"

"Of course the people elected them."

"Call them the ordinary citizens," said the
Judge. "I like your term. They are where the law
comes from, you see. For they chose the delegates who made the Constitution that provided
for the courts. There's your machinery. These
are the hands into which ordinary citizens have
put the law." . . . But "[t]he courts, or rather the
juries, into whose hands we have put the law, are
not dealing the law. They are withered hands, or
rather they are imitation hands made for show,
with no life in them, no grip. They cannot hold a
cattle-thief. And so when your ordinary citizen
sees this, and sees that he has placed justice in a
dead hand, he must take justice back into his
own hands where it was once at the beginning of
all things. Call this primitive, if you will. But so
far from being a defiance of the law, it is an assertion of it — the fundamental assertion of self-
governing men, upon whom our whole social
fabric is based. There is your principle, Miss
Wood, as I see it. Now can you help me to see
anything different?"

She could not.

"But perhaps you are of the same opinion still?"
the Judge inquired.

"It is all terrible to me," she said.

"Yes; and so is capital punishment terrible. And
so is war. And perhaps some day we shall do
without them. But they are none of them so terrible as unchecked theft and murder would be."

An accumulation of betrayals, both legal and moral,

has delivered America to a place where ersatz justice is entrenched against Americans. What was once a frontier that briefly achieved civilization has been corrupted from within to subvert the *meaning* of civilization. The hands into which Americans placed the law have overwhelmingly become hands made for show, hands working not to protect Americans from criminals but to sandbag the supreme law that protects Americans from criminals — *especially government criminals.*

There is no original-Constitution provision to support the presumed "doctrine of sovereign immunity," although in 1795 Congress took its first stab at resuscitating the Divine Right of Kings-presumption that a Sovereign, i.e., the government, can do no wrong — probably in fearful response to the first U.S. Supreme Court Chief Justice's finding that a citizen *can* sue the government. A diminished Supreme Court has since repeatedly upheld the position that the government cannot be sued *without its consent.* "The universally received opinion is that no suit can be commenced or prosecuted against the United States" wrote Chief Justice John Marshall in 1821. In 1834 he added, " . . . as the United States is not suable of common right, the party who institutes such suit must bring his case within the authority of some act of Congress, or the court cannot exercise jurisdiction over it."

Owen Wister was right in 1902. He is right today.

When ordinary citizens see that they have placed justice in a dead hand, they must take justice back into their own hands where it was once at the beginning of all things. The affirmation of this principle is not a defiance of the law, but an assertion of it — the fundamental assertion of self-governing men.

Civilization, the foundation of which is objective, impartial, rights-protecting law, cannot otherwise exist.

PUBLIC ENEMY #2:

NORMALCY BIAS

Normalcy bias — the "It can't happen here" or "It can't happen to me" syndrome — causes people to underestimate or deny the possibility of disaster, natural or man-made. Since a particular disaster has not been experienced by a particular person, the assumption that it never will be experienced becomes manifest and often widespread, a normalcy *virus*. Whether applying to the private realm — illness, accident, divorce, job loss, bankruptcy, substance addiction, and every variety of personal undoing — or to global catastrophe, the recipe for normalcy bias is probably as old as humanity itself. Wishful thinking, restricted vision, ignorance of history, failure or unwillingness to objectively credit evidence, and inattentiveness combine to assure the comfortably unaware that everything's fine.

In the political realm, thinking otherwise and saying so is certain to subject even the most reasonable skeptic to accusations of being a paranoid, an alarmist, a fearmonger, and to that punishment dreaded most of all: ostracism and ridicule.

Despite the warning signs in 1930s Germany — including Adolf Hitler's publication of a book foretelling his intentions[1] — Germans remained in denial before, during, and after their elected Chief National Socialist's delivery of intended atrocities. Concentration camps? Mandatory sterilization? Forced medical experimentation? *Their* government's murder of millions?

"No one would do that," so many believed. "That can't happen here," echoed an unshakable normalcy bias.

And while those brave enough to offer warnings were denounced as paranoids and traitors to the Fatherland, deadly gas manufactured by prominent German industrialists was being pumped into the lungs of men, women, and children who believed that their masters were leading them, accompanied by lilting melodies from *The Merry Widow* and *Tales of Hoffman*, to public showers.

Two decades later, once the CIA and FBI coined the term to defame anyone challenging the lies surrounding the assassination of John F. Kennedy, similar paranoid harbingers of prescient warning would be branded "conspiracy theorists."

"Denial," wrote Iris Chang, "is an integral part of atrocity, and it's a natural part after a society has committed genocide. First you kill, and then the memory of killing is killed."[2]

The actions of Hitler's Third Reich are merely, if such a word can be used anywhere near round-the-clock incineration chambers and mass graves, the most publicized example of a psychopath and his minions advocating and performing a collective cleansing by murder. Of course, we assure ourselves, the government genocide of 150 million human beings in the twentieth century happened in uncivilized dictator-oppressed far-off lands such as China,

Cambodia, Guatemala, Bosnia, Chile, Rhodesia, and the old Soviet Union.

That can't happen *here*.

And besides, if it was happening here we would be reading about it in the newspaper and watching it on television. *The New York Times* and *Washington Post* would be investigating relentlessly and headlining the truth. Our awesomely intellectual, fashionably dressed, makeup-artist groomed, enviably overpaid friends at the BBC, CNN, MSNBC, CBS, ABC, and Fox would be reporting on it nightly from behind their status-affirming desks or, more empathetically, from a homey semi-circle of chatting pals with their legs crossed *just so* and their tresses arranged in perfect spiraling cascades over their collarbones.

Well, no, they wouldn't. Per their corporate check-writers and government masters they would be massaging their dedicated audience members' tenacious adherence to "that can't happen here."

Doug Hagmann wrote in *Canada Free Press*, "The problem is that most people are not thinking large enough, nor do they understand the magnitude of the lie. Many will die from what is coming. The level of evil behind this plan is incomprehensible to the normal human mind."

Cue normalcy bias.

Whether Mr. Hagmann was referencing Mao's China, Stalin's Russia, Hitler's Germany, or the *real* reason for Covid-ruse-legitimized worldwide business closures, face-canceling mandates, and compulsory vaccination makes no difference. Most people do not think large enough. Most can neither understand nor accept the magnitude of government-propagated lies, no matter how often or how clearly history reveals past truths. Such evil *is* incomprehensible to the normal mind. Add to incomprehensibility the chorus of a thousand human parrots all squawking the message in unison and one can choose from a list of metaphors to describe the result. Lemmings on parade. Tailgating into a pileup. Lambs to the slaughter. Follow the leader. One neck for one leash.

But even if evil were not at play, even if the parrots were not all squawking from a script penned for the purpose of advancing a dark agenda, inattentiveness and lack of vision alone are enough to give normalcy bias an unshakable foothold — a foothold strong enough to utterly disable independent discernment.

Isabel Paterson said it best eighty-one years ago in *The God of the Machine*:[3]

> . . . when men have become engrossed in practical devices they are apt to narrow their field of vision and lose sight of the interconnection of the various branches of knowledge. More than that . . . they will even forget the larger principles they have applied, and on which their well-being depends.

Cue the second component of Juvenal's "bread and circus games" depiction of Rome between the fall of the Republic and the rise of the Empire: the range-of-the-moment amusements by which an entire citizenry may be kept passively occupied and distracted.[4]

I have long been bewildered by stories and songs that depict a personal awakening after tragedy, a slap-in-the-face realization of the fragility and value of life when on the verge of losing it. Someone dies unexpectedly and of a sudden the story-teller/song-singer realizes it's time to live a fuller life, climb a mountain, learn to skydive, take more chances, appreciate his children, love his wife better, drink a little less beer, work a little harder — poetic renditions of awakenings from normalcy bias, often to be followed by a return to normalcy bias, albeit at an adjusted take-the-good-for-granted level.

How, with life on display all around us and with history ever-more-conveniently at our fingertips, does an awakening from normalcy bias so often come only on the brink of loss?

In America and around the world, but most pointedly in advanced nations, normalcy bias has been methodically exploited and expanded into a new politically contrived realm: the normalization of abnormality, immorality, and evil. What began as an observable amplification of violence in movies and television — and then in video games and in a popular low form of music — was but a foot in the door for the yet-to-come. Commensurate with the Left's campaign of reality denial and concept redefinition is a frenetic crusade to transform the unacceptable into the acceptable, the repugnant into the humdrum, the insane into the every-day, the "never in my lifetime" into the "I don't like it but what can I do?"

Specifically: forced business closures; medical coercion; the politicization of race, sex, religion, health, science, justice; in-your-face judiciary corruption; election fraud; foreign-government blackmail, bribery, influence peddling; pedophilia;[5] violent "peaceful" protests; biological self-reidentification; government reidentification of rights as privileges; replacement migration through intentionally porous national borders; replacement parenting through government intrusion and compulsion; hypocrisy flaunted like some higher means of expression; language made contradictory and meaningless.

Cue normalcy *redefinition*.

Teach it to the parrots. Insinuate it into law. Wield it

like a club. Combine it with normalcy bias and the result is a formula for self-destruction no less potent than hydrogen cyanide but undetectable in an autopsy.

Those who sense that something is wrong will never identify the "something" in time to protect themselves and their loved ones without decisively overriding normalcy bias.

"But," one might reasonably ask, "how can we separate ourselves from a condition integral to the human experience, a condition easy to assume and difficult to recognize?"

The answer is in two parts.

First, since we cannot process information we are prevented from seeing, we must zoom out to see more, to discover what may be hidden by the anointed Guardians of Truth.

Normalcy bias in the political realm is reinforced en masse within the dominant mantra, the narrative most fervently repeated by the propaganda parrots, the one on every popular channel. A telltale indicator that the message is wrong is when it intimates a personal deficiency: If *you* don't agree then there is something wrong with *you*.

We must switch to fundamentally different channels, to channels not beholden to regime or corporate-sponsor interests, to channels disparaged by the parrots. We must realize that when the parrots' propaganda is threatened their squawking gets louder and their disparagement more uniform. (For a laughably obvious illustration, rewind to and replay the Joe Rogan-Ivermectin hysteria.) We must realize that when the parrots squawk for censorship it is because the parrots know that their propaganda is certain to fail rational argument.

Second, since we cannot evaluate objectively through a lens distorted by prejudice, preconceived notions, bias, peer pressure, assumptions of duty, obedience, dogma, fear, or an everything's-fine filter, we must employ a lens free from such defects. To prepare that lens, we can each ask of ourselves and honestly answer one question:

What is my foremost talent?

Am I good at managing people, time, or money? At solving problems? Communicating ideas? What makes me a competent carpenter? Parent? Caregiver? Soldier? Athlete? Artist? Teacher? Doctor? Chess player? What particular attributes make me good at some particular thing I do?

Anyone with the ability to independently identify and put to beneficial use the principles that constitute an earnest personal endeavor can apply this specialty-specific talent to a bigger picture, to a world beyond the specialty. Anyone who has ever relied upon independent thinking, which is a literal redundancy, for the accomplishment of a specialty-specific goal can call upon that thinking for broader application.

Are you willing to widen your vision to include the bigger picture and to apply to that bigger picture the independence of mind that makes you good at your specialty? Do you value what remains of your time on earth? Do you respect it as *yours*?

Life is a terminal event. Happiness is elusive. Should we risk foreshortening the first while hoping the second will fall across our paths when it is within our power to safeguard our one opportunity "to be or not to be" by owning "to see or not to see"? Is it so difficult to choose independent awareness and self-responsibility while immersed in an interdependent culture of more, easier, faster, "free"? Must tragedy be the alarm that stirs us from the slumber induced by circus games and normalcy bias?

No. No. And, no.

What did we learn from the Covid ruse?[6]

Did we learn that face masks, despite a century of sci-
entific and medical research, were suddenly able to prevent the passage of alleged viral particles vastly smaller
than the pores through which breath must pass? Or that
standing six feet from our neighbors kept us safe from the
danger lurking inside our neighbors? Or that the forced
closure of thousands of businesses accomplished anything
but the destruction of livelihoods, lives, and dreams? Or
that a test incapable of detecting illness suddenly, by an act
of sheer government will, transformed itself into a universally accepted barometer of illness? Or that the disappear-
ance of the flu was not the result of its redesignation as
something else? Or that a government-tenured medical
despot with an audacious record of science-manipulation,
fear-peddling, position flip-flopping, and pharmaceutical
profiteering suddenly discovered morality and became a
Prophet of Medical Truth? Or that rushed, insufficiently
tested, fraudulently documented, gene-manipulating coerced injections redefined as "vaccines" were safe and effective?

When the next manufactured pandemic accidentally
comes around, will we tilt back our heads and offer our
nostrils to assault? Push our neighbors away in fear? Lock
ourselves in our homes? Strap on face diapers? Accept
some politician's decree that what some of us do as productive human beings is *nonessential?* Will we destroy our
livelihoods? Roll up our sleeves for booster-number whatever? Post selfies on social media displaying our injection
wounds? Acquiesce to vaccine passports and social-credit
scores installed on our phones or tattooed across our foreheads or inserted under our skin?

What will we think — *what will we do* — when the
World Health Organization is unconstitutionally granted
authority[7] *by our government* not merely over our national

sovereignty but over personal sovereignty? What will we do when we receive in the mail, free, of course, a twelve-month supply of masks and next-pandemic self-testing kits? And unigender antibacterial jerseys with shoulder-access flaps? And Bureau of Disinformation-approved hearing protectors. And conspiracy-theory-blocking rose-colored eyewear? And the first of our regime-guaranteed Universal Basic Income checks?

What will we do when we finally understand the actual planned meaning of "new normal"? When we glimpse the goal of normalcy redefinition massaged into normalcy bias?

Those who remain in denial or who believe they can survive what is coming by playing along are likely even to deny the door slamming shut on their forsaken opportunity. Screams of "I did not know" or "I couldn't help it" or "This can't be happening here" from the wrong side of that door will not reopen it, although such screams may serve to muffle the distant echo of the paranoid, the alarmist, the fearmonger, the conspiracy theorist still reasonably offering from the land of the ostracized and unheeded history:

We tried to tell you.

PUBLIC ENEMY #1:
PUBLIC EDUCATION

*"Give me four years to teach the children
and the seed I have sown will never be uprooted."*

Vladimir Ilyich Lenin

The principles responsible for the creation of America are, and have always been, required in equal measure to sustain America. Only an independent-minded citizenry can preserve a free independent nation. America's founders understood this, but America's enemies understood it as well and long ago set in motion a patient plan to sabotage The Founders' vision. By incessantly nudging American public education toward an anti-reason, anti-liberty benchmark, authoritarians on either side of the false political divide have at last brought to fruition the prerequisite for a post-America dictatorship: a nation of citizens unable to think independently.

The earliest American schools attained the educational ideal necessary for maintaining a literate, thinking citizenry. Their focus on the teaching of fundamentals — reading, writing, arithmetic — was not because life in the nineteenth century was uncomplicated, but because developing in children the ability to reason and a solid base of essential knowledge in preparation for life as adults *requires only the teaching of fundamentals.*

Then and now.

The complexities of life in the twentieth and twenty-first centuries neither demand nor excuse making education the complicated, politicized, teach-'em-everything mess it is today because education is not vocational or career or specialty training. Education is what provides the foundation for vocational, career, and specialty training and, as such, must be strictly limited to subjects and lessons that provide that foundation.

For details too expansive to summarize, I recommend *Honor Student*,[1] previously referenced. From the perspectives of an inquisitive high-school senior and the reclusive ex-teacher he befriends, the novel explores the role of reason in education. Upon their second encounter the embittered former educator tells the student:

> "I spoke to you because it seemed there might be a chance for your mind to survive their system. I apologize for my rudeness just now. You asked Rebecca why I quit teaching? Ask first, what is required of learning? What is the purpose of education? What social, political, and economic conditions presuppose the existence of a proper educational system? Contrast the answers to those questions with the concept of public schooling, and you'll see the reason for the distance between what education should be and what it has become."

By the story's conclusion the student understands his inability to obediently accept what he is told he must know, and why in government-controlled education the most important and *most human* of all questions is stigmatized, ignored, or forbidden.

The earliest government-school manipulators would be overjoyed to witness today's rightfully angry parents challenging Critical Race Theory, Inspired Gender Confusion, and Politically Correct History. Not because the teaching of absurdities was these manipulators' specific goal, but because their goal — the destruction of reason as a tool for independent human life — has today been achieved so successfully that absurdities are considered debate-worthy.

They would be overjoyed, but not surprised, because the debacle was inevitable. As H.L. Mencken observed a century ago:[2]

> "That erroneous assumption is to the effect that the aim of public education is to fill the young of the species with knowledge and awaken their intelligence, and so make them fit to discharge the duties of citizenship in an enlightened and independent manner. Nothing could be further from the truth.
>
> "The aim of public education is not to spread enlightenment at all; it is simply to reduce as many individuals as possible to the same safe level, to breed and train a standardized citizenry, to put down dissent and originality. That is its aim in the United States, whatever the pretensions of politicians, pedagogues, and other such mountebanks, and that is its aim everywhere else."

While parents and the best of their elected representatives demand "change," their demands are in response to
fruit from seeds deeply planted and thoroughly rooted, to
a more-bitter-than-usual crop from a tree that has for
generations been nourished by parents and their elected
representatives. School-board-meeting speeches against
[fill in the blank] may be justified and motivational, but
that [fill in the blank] is not the problem and removing it
from the classroom is not the solution. "Pushing back"
against education's most brazen contemporary offenses is
far too little, far too late.

Government control over the most important years
of an individual's development is an irreversible step toward the destruction of freedom in society. Public Enemy
Number One, regardless of professed good intentions, is
public education.

Of course there are within this corruptible-by-design
system, good teachers. It is largely because of their influence that some students graduate relatively unindoctri-
nated. But make no mistake: those who emerge from
government-controlled education still capable of independent thinking do so not *because* of the system, but *in
spite of it*. And with every passing year it becomes more
and more difficult for good teachers to survive as good
teachers within this corruptible-by-design system.

An American future requires the complete disman-
tling and from-scratch rebuilding of educational curriculum, methodology, and goals. Practically speaking, this
will necessitate a years-long commitment to closing public
schools, eliminating the Department of Education and
politicized teachers' unions, and independently schooling
children until every one of 98,000 Institutions for Conceptual Pacification has been replaced by private Centers
for Education.

The only way to protect children from cognitive sub-version and ruin is to teach by example that questioning what they are told until it has been proven sensible is not only every student's job, but every child's first right on the road to adulthood. And the only way to implement such a protection is to renounce the supremely fallacious assumption that government should have anything to do with teaching children the essential tool for distinguishing between sensible ideas and senseless authority.

More personally to the point: If *you* are happy with America's current direction, by all means give thanks to public education and trust your children to the future it promises and is magnificently achieving. If you are unhappy, you must remove your children from public education's influence and protest the taxes extorted from you for its perpetuation.

To do less will fail to reestablish even the fact that two plus two equals four. To do less will handcuff the best pro-America political policies to their destroyer. To do less will guarantee a future of vacant faces staring into screens flashing an announcement that even the most successfully dumbed-down public-school progeny can appreciate:

Game Over.

Moral good can never lastingly prevail over evil through political action because politics is merely a conse-quence of philosophy — of what people value, how they think, how they were taught to think. Politics is the hand that responds to prevailing philosophy. Education is the power that shapes the mind that shapes the philosophy that directs the hand. It is the wellspring from which a nation ascends, or the quagmire into which it sinks.

Lenin's "Дайте мне четыре года, чтобы научить детей, и семя, которое я посеял, никогда не будет вырвано с корнем" is a truism applicable to both good and evil results in any language, but when implemented by political authority it will sooner or later serve the inclination of political authority. It will, as Mencken assured, function "to reduce as many individuals as possible to the same safe level, to breed and train a standardized" — and compliant — "citizenry."

And it will result in what Soviet *Novosti Press Agency* propagandist Yuri Bezmenov ("Tomas Schuman" after defection) warned in his 1984 "Love Letter to America."[3]

> The Western public seldom receives the explanation of the price of the state-controlled Socialist-type education: political conformity to dictatorship, ideological brainwashing, lack of individual initiative in "educated masses."
>
> The American romance with state-run education as encouraged by KGB subverters has already produced generations of graduates who cannot spell, cannot find Nicaragua on a world map, cannot think creatively and independently.
>
> The eventual result is very predictable: ignorance combined with anti-Americanism.

Until "honor student" represents not a government's stamp of approval but a personal badge earned for life by independent reasoning minds, America can never again exist as America because:

> *Only an independent-minded citizenry*
> *can preserve a free independent nation.*

CENSORSHIP'S SWINDLING COUSIN
AND THE SIMPLEST WORD
IN THE WORLD

Independent-media providers have abundantly spot-lighted an increasingly obvious plan to control global populations by means of currency manipulation, food-supply disruptions, and travel restrictions. With the exception of health-care tyranny and censorship, both of which America and the world experienced like a tsunami throughout the Covid ruse, there is nothing more effective at controlling people than curtailing their ability to trade, feed, and move. But a far more insidious tool for manipu-lation is a blood-relative of censorship sufficiently subtle to escape detection when viewed in the moment.

Twelve years ago, a young Canadian composer in my employ attempted to calm my anger over the repeated misuse of an important word by some politician we were hearing in a radio interview. After I silenced the contrap-tion he said, "It's okay. English is a living language."

And so it is — but not in the way my musician friend implied nor in the way many modern linguists insist. To the extent that language shares with living organisms some of the characteristics of living organisms — birth, growth, maturation, adaptability, strength derived from focused use, atrophy resulting from disuse, the capacity for reproduction, cross-breeding, interbreeding, and evolution — language *is* alive. But just as life cannot for long be sustained in a state of contradiction, neither can language if it is intended to be used as a tool for communication and understanding, rather than as a tool for creating uncertainty, confusion, and chaos.

In a June 2020 article published in *The Atlantic*, linguist John McWhorter wrote about the definition of racism:[1]

> Dictionaries can lag behind societal developments, and the idea that a "word" indisputably "means" what dictionaries say is simply sloppy. Words' meanings change inevitably and constantly, and not just in terms of slang. Anyone who doubts that might take a listen to how people use the word fantastic in old episodes of *The Twilight Zone* or old movies, when they meant not "Great!" but what we would now express as "fantastical." The change was gradual. But here, in the real, non-fantastical world, people tend to think that the cold print of dictionaries implies some kind of unchanging truth. As such, it won't do for definitions of words as crucial as racism to sit frozen somewhere around the era of Watergate and fondue. We've come a long way, baby.

And so we have, Mr. McWhorter — many miles down the wrong road.

Words are created to represent objects, actions, ideas,

and conditions both in singular application and when combined in phrases, sentences, paragraphs, chapters, and tomes. If language is to be employed as a tool for communication and understanding, precision and agreed-upon definitions are paramount. If for the purpose of sowing uncertainty, confusion, and chaos: meaning-malleability, misapplication, and impermanence reign.

The linguist continued:

> Editors at Merriam-Webster are working on a revision of the definition of racism. So the Great Awokening is even going so far as to change the dictionary? Not quite — sociopolitics drew the usage of the word *racism* beyond the dictionary definition long ago, and it is high time our dictionaries got the message.

Racism, Mr. McWhorter proposes, must no longer mean what it once meant because society and politicians have been using it to mean something else and, therefore, in response to sociopolitical meaning-stretching, dictionaries must rewrite their description of the word in favor of its *mis*application.

By this rationale, the longstanding misuse of words such as liberty, rights, capitalism, pragmatism, democracy, republic, justice, science, man, and reality warrants not a correction of the misuse out of respect for concept designation and communicative consistency, but a redefining in the service of uncertainty, confusion, and chaos. Contrary to societal misuse and political manipulation, liberty is not tyranny in moderation. Rights are not privileges bestowed by government. Capitalism is not enterprise by bureaucrat permission. Pragmatism is not "practical realism." Justice is not multi-tiered. Science is not consensus. America is not a democracy. Man, as the word derives from *human* and relates to *mankind*, is neither male nor female. Reality is not negotiable — regardless of suggested, ordered, or published dictionary revisions.

And although language does share many of its characteristics with living organisms, respect for language requires that it be maintained according to the same reality-based limitations common to living organisms. A dog cannot at the same time be a fish — even if it loves to swim. An eye cannot be a tail. Freedom is not slavery.

Mr. McWhorter sagely observes that "[t]he conceptual step between a healthy person and a healthy society is a short one, as is that between a racist person and a racist society," but the truth of his statement derives from the meaning of the concepts he references. If their definitions are subject to sociopolitical whim, it is pointless even to discuss health and racism because "health" today can be "racism" tomorrow. A dog that swims can be a fish. A man who wears a bra can be a chest-feeding birthing person. And definitions with moral or political implication become George Orwell's "blackwhite."

Those who know *Nineteen Eighty-Four* only as a movie should consider the conceptual and societal consequences of word-meaning redesignation as explained by Orwell in his novel's appendix (*Ingsoc* is the Party's name for English Socialism).[2]

> The purpose of Newspeak was not only to provide a medium of expression for the world-view and mental habits proper to the devotees of Ingsoc, but to make all other modes of thought impossible. It was intended that when Newspeak had been adopted once and for all and Oldspeak forgotten, a heretical thought — that is, a thought

diverging from the principles of Ingsoc —
should be literally unthinkable, at least as far as
thought is dependent on words. Its vocabulary
was so constructed as to give exact and often
very subtle expression to every meaning that a
Party member could properly wish to express,
while excluding all other meanings and also the
possibility of arriving at them by indirect meth-
ods. This was done partly by the invention of
new words, but chiefly by eliminating undesir-
able words and by stripping such words as remained of unorthodox meaning, and so far as
possible of all secondary meanings whatever. To
give a single example: The word "free" still
existed in Newspeak, but it could only be used in
such statements as "This dog is free from lice" or
"This field is free from weeds." It could not be
used in its old sense of "politically free" or
"intellectually free," since political and intellectual freedom no longer existed even as concepts, and were therefore of necessity nameless.

This is fiction achievable in reality even without the
aid of artificial so-called "intelligence." It has been in process for decades and is accelerating daily.

The key to communicating effectively with another
human being — and thereby harmoniously arriving at understanding — is to do so as precisely as possible using
language that consists of established terminology. Likewise, the key to creating uncertainty, confusion, and chaos
— and thereby priming another human being, or an entire
society, for manipulation and control — is to do so as
capriciously and contradictorily as possible using language
intentionally rendered meaningless.

Words have long been used as weapons — the might of the pen versus the might of the sword, as it were — by men and women who respect the value of words assembled meaningfully for the purpose of prevailing in a dispute. What we are seeing today, however, is the deliberate misuse and destruction of words for the purpose of prevailing not with open rational discourse and not even with the threat of a sword wielded in daylight, but with a smothering pillow deployed during slumber. This duplicitous weapon is made possible by those who have incrementally acquiesced to the fads and trends imposed upon language, and to the betrayal of meaning. A preponderance of novelists, editors, publishers, essayists, journalists, advertising-copy writers, historians, linguists, teachers, playwrights, and even legal scholars — professionals who should have stood fast as guardians of meaning — have willingly and pathetically assented.

If the script appeals to the masses — even if inaccurate, illiterate, or linguistically misleading — it's good to go. Woe unto the author, editor, or publisher who expects readers to rise to an un-dumbed-down piece of prose.

Over time, language narrows, minds shrink, comprehension contracts, understanding is traded for uncritical acceptance, and those who would use words to manipulate and control seize their opportunity. It is usually not politician stupidity that causes laws to be written in language impossible to comprehend; confusing laws accommodate desired arbitrary enforcement.

English has been transformed throughout its history by both subtle and colossal influences. Germanic-tribe invasion in the fifth century replaced Celtic with Englisc; Christianity's introduction of parchment eclipsed the use of wood, bone, and stone for writing; the Norman invasion of the mid-eleventh century brought Anglo-Norman,

Anglo-Saxon, Latin, and French into use; and by the thirteenth century British authors and parliament were employing what is now called Middle English. The Renaissance elevated the use of Latin and Greek while Shakespeare originated words and phrases that would result in new pronunciations and The Great Vowel Shift; the printing press was invented in 1439 and, for the relative few who could read, the first dictionary was published 165 years later. In the eighteenth and nineteenth centuries, and through the first half of the twentieth, the American and Industrial Revolutions plus two world wars opened the floodgates.

Progressively efficient modes of transportation and communication, mass goods-and-weapons production, energy development, evolving venues for entertainment, the creation and rise of the pharmaceutical industry, the globalization of politics — all required a significant expansion of language. The late twentieth century's information-age achievements saw "news" and drug-prescribed health care become big business and a light-speed transition to dependence upon computer technology — more new words for new concepts.

And in the early twenty-first century . . .

The life stages of English — commonly designated Early, Middle, Early Modern, and Late Modern — so far correspond with the life stages of human beings and civilizations, from birth through late maturity. Judging by the acceleration of language defilement over the past twenty years, the coming stage of English may well be its last. When language is divorced from reality — when it consists of floating interchangeable constructs — when it simultaneously expresses anything and nothing — when an advanced nation's president and vice president can publicly mumble incoherently and spew unintelligible gibberish without being booed from the stage — when the nonfiction equivalent of Newspeak is bandied about in pretend scholarly discussions — when word butchery and meaning murder are accepted and propagated by writers, publishers, media outlets, college professors, and governments — what we are hearing and reading is not the expansion of living language, but a death rattle and obituary.

Sooner or later, every hidden destructive force must come into the light to claim its prize. The English language, mutely suffering in lazy decline, is now openly being transformed from a tool for communication and understanding to a tool for creating uncertainty, confusion, and chaos. It is a grand coming-out of censorship's swindling cousin, a ne'er do well whose maleficence is accomplished not by silencing speech and burning books, but by stealing, and then murdering, meaning.

This thought-constricting, concept-destroying subversion of language could have been prevented, perhaps can still be reversed, by calling upon the simplest and single-most uncorruptible word in any language — the word most likely to be the last redefined by sociopolitical sway — the word that honorably exemplifies an unpoliticized definition of extremist. By saying and meaning:

No.

5

CENSORSHIP'S SWINDLING COUSIN
AND THE MURDER OF MEANING

There are, of course, those who do not
want us to speak. I suspect even now orders are
being shouted into telephones and men with
guns will soon be on their way. Why?

Because while the truncheon may be used
in lieu of conversation, words will always retain
their power. Words offer the means to meaning and
for those who will listen, the annunciation of truth.
And the truth is: There is something terribly
wrong with this country, isn't there?

V for Vendetta

If I expected people to give me their trust or follow my
advice or obey my orders because I hold a PhD or because I've published multiple peer-reviewed papers or
because I'm the director of the World Health Organization
— or a Hollywood star who once acted the part of an honorable character — or a familiar talking head acting the

part of a journalist — or the latest White House press secretary — I would be flaunting disdain for my audience. If I held such an expectation while mouthing what I was told to say or what I knew to be false or misleading, my work would be a lie. And if my work was built not upon my fellow human beings' strengths — intelligence, integrity, mature powers of discernment — but upon their weaknesses — ignorance, gullibility, a predilection to be deceived — my life would be a lie. In every way that matters I would be lower than the least enlightened of all human beings because my "success" would derive from my ability to sell and perpetuate unenlightenment.

Although some of the world's most successful liars are bedecked with the trappings of power and wealth, for as long as they live no remuneration or purloined reputation will alter the fact that they are con men, fraudsters, parasites, and vampires. Only by appealing to the highest intellectual and moral virtues in their fellow human beings can they be worthy of respect. Only by demonstrating the truth of their words can their positions and titles be honorably earned.

Only by recognizing and affirming that what matters is not *who*, but *true,* can you and I defend our health, happiness, liberty, and lives.

But what if the language we need to
communicate truth has for decades been, and is
this very minute being, rendered meaningless?

CENSORSHIP IS THE MOST powerful method of controlling thought because what we perceive of "unauthorized" information, whether expurgated by Ministry of Truth-employee scissors or AI programming, is this:

We cannot evaluate or even contemplate what we are
prevented from seeing and hearing. We cannot know what
we are prevented from knowing. But censorship is not the
only malevolent player in the war against thought, knowledge, and independent life; it is merely the most disrep-
utable of a four-member gang.

The Censor silences and suppresses.

The Propagandist lies and misleads.

The Thief of Meaning redefines and eventually kills.

Consensual Conscripts acquiesce as a population and,
while helping to institutionalize normalcy bias, grant destructive power to a trio of fiends otherwise powerless.

The Censor and The Propagandist are today receiv-
ing more and more attention as they become desperate to

protect the authoritarian-collectivist narrative. Sooner or later, every hidden destructive force must come into the light to claim its prize — aggressively so when the prize is resisting. Although by contrast The Thief of Meaning remains for the most part in the shadows, he has been diligently active in America ever since liars gained a podium. And although The Thief redefines for political expediency words like terrorist, insurrection, racist, antisemitism, Nazi, and extremist — and for fun serves up absurdities like "birthing person," "minor-attracted person," "biological man," and "health food" — such offerings are peripheral to a long-term mission less obvious than that of his cohorts and deliberately transitionally palatable.

Instrumental in subverting the proper relationship between individual citizens and government is the manipulated evolution of the word "public." Public safety, public housing, public education, public interest, public health, public policy, public opinion, and public good effectively nullify the primacy of the individual. Although most dictionary definitions of the word are politically neutral — "the people as a whole" and "a group of people having common interests" — the concept is elevated to deity status and exploited to eclipse the rights of individuals.

Grouping singular men and women into a collective whole is the primary tenet of collectivism, and defining this whole as having "common interests" obscures and diminishes independent sovereign identity. "Public opinion" is a meaningless manipulable cliché. "Public health" is no more valid a concept than "public stomach." "For the public good" has for centuries justified expropriating wealth, property, ideas, liberty, and life. Notably, since "public education" has little to do with educating and everything to do with shaping a "public," as a label it boasts a certain twisted sensibility.

Are *you* a "member of the public" if you vehemently stand against "public opinion"? What if some coercive government policy in the name of "public safety" jeopardized *your* safety? Would refusal to comply disqualify you from "public membership"?

The notion of public property is self-negating, contradicting both the meaning of ownership and the right to use what is allegedly owned. Property "owned" by a theoretical everyone is owned by no one, and those chosen to oversee the management and disposition of the property in question answer not to a fictitious "everyone" — who as individuals are compelled via taxation to foot the bill — but to an agenda-directed chosen few.

Words are routinely and deliberately misused to downplay, exaggerate, and otherwise "adjust" facts of reality, usually to gain something the misuser lacks the courage or integrity to gain legitimately. Addressing Xi Jinping or Kim Jong Un as "leaders" of their respective dictator-oppressed nations diminishes what it means to lead. And since the English definition of president does not apply to foreign despots who call themselves "presidents," even conversationally granting despots such a title defiles the term.

Coextensively, when Ronald Reagan referred in a speech to Communist China as "so-called Communist China" he unjustly downplayed a brutal political system and rendered morally vacant his subsequent branding of the Soviet Union as an "evil empire." (Regardless of the likelihood that both phrases were authored not by Reagan, but by a speech writer.)

Is such criticism merely picking at nits? Or do accuracy and defensibility matter when an individual with power and influence takes the stage and commands an audience?

Capitalism is not a combination of market freedom and government controls, of private-purchase choice and bureaucrat favor. It is not business conducted courtesy of political permission or regulatory manipulation or bankruptcy rescue via taxpayer bailouts. And, yet, a system no government has ever allowed to exist according to its *laissez-faire* definition gets blamed for every failure caused by government.

In a nation where government serves rather than reigns, there is no such thing as "the private sector." In such a nation, private life is not categorized as an exception and assigned a "sector."

Americans have an inalienable right to *liberty* — not to "liberties." The nonchalant pluralization of what was once America's distinguishing and most-illustrious virtue betrays its unpoliticized meaning by chopping a singular principle into portions for distribution.

Government-controlled media outlets parrot the regime's narrative even when it contradicts last year's or yesterday's script. Simple words with simple definitions like voluntary, mandatory, science, male, female, racism, justice, choice, patriot, protester, and traitor are intentionally distorted and transformed into political artillery while meaning-impoverished constructs like living wage, white privilege, hate crime, pro-lifer, anti-vaxxer, conspiracy theorist, fill-in-the-blank denier, violence-inciter, domestic terrorist, and disinformation spreader are made trendy as labels and deployed as argument silencers. Among the beneficiaries of this effrontery are the IRS, EPA, USDA, FDA, NHS, DHS, NSA, CIA, and FBI, all of which rely on undefined, misdefined, and redefined terms to arbitrarily enforce subjective interpretations of law.

America is not a democracy, but a constitutional republic. The widespread misapplication of the word by politicians, bureaucrats, judges, educators, journalists, and media personalities of every political persuasion creates with repetition, whether deliberate or negligent, a trickle-down concept-demolishing effect.

The word *rights* — six letters that combine to represent the most crucial safeguard of human life — has been so obscenely misused, definition-stretched, legally eviscerated, and officially rendered self-contradictory that it can now serve as the poster child of meaning murder. There is no such thing as a right to a *thing*, to a product or service or idea, unless the claimant is also the creator of that product, service, or idea. There is no right to education, healthcare, clean water, an opinion podium, a living wage, or a basic income. There is only the right to pursue — free from force and fraud, including and especially by government — the rights-respecting creation and acquisition of these and similar values. To suggest that anyone has a right to infringe upon the rights of another is to annihilate the concept of rights, and the popular practice of segregating and parceling rights into women's, worker's, gun-owner's, parental, medical, minority, migrant, student, tenant, trans, voter, and pedestrian serves the same purpose as making liberty and freedom plural: to compartmentalize, divide, and diminish the overarching principle of what the word *rights* represents.

The casually tossed-about phrase "critical thinking" implies that there is some other kind of thinking, when there is not. To think "uncritically" is not to think, but to engage in something that is not thinking. "Critical thinking" is a redundancy that assures those who do not process information conceptually and independently that they are still somehow thinking, when they are not — despite encouragement by *The New York Times*. "Independent thinking" is similarly redundant, and although useful as a term to inspire the self-processed discovery and ownership of ideas and opinions, it implies that there is such a thing as collective thinking, when there is not — despite encouragement by collectivists and AI promoters. Individuals can agree, collaborate, and conspire at will, but the result of their cooperative thoughtful effort still derives from individual minds grasping and integrating concepts.

Add to this burgling of important words the vacuous swapping-out of allegedly offensive terms for milder versions — which, of course, changes nothing about the concepts they represent — and we have meaning tweaking as a useful distraction for those whose brains are small enough to apoplectically obsess over "chairman," "handicapped," "forefather," "blacklisted," "slum," "sportsmanship," "deaf," "maid," "fat," "waitress," and "blind."

The patient piddling achievements by The Thief of Meaning, as well as those more imperiously pursued by The Censor and The Propagandist, would be impossible without the endorsement and participation of Consensual Conscripts — the unaware, unquestioning, normalcy-bias-embracing, go-along-to-get-along pragmaticians whose capacity for acceptance and thoughtless repetition is as reliable as sunrise.

How can those who float through life on autopilot — content to believe, trust, and obey authority — be expected to dispute or even notice the misuse of a word like democracy? How can those who are happy to buy, do, and swallow what their friends, family, and coworkers buy, do, and swallow be expected to feel indignant when corralled into a pen under a sign that reads: "The General Public"? How can those who are afraid of ostracism be expected to challenge the U.S. Department of Education's implementation of education? How can those who are more concerned with *appearing* to do right than with *doing* right be

expected to say, "I own this house. I do not need some bureaucrat's permission to add a porch to it."

How can those who are steeped in self-sacrifice, duty,
and obedience be expected to raise a finger, or even an
eyebrow, when their neighbors are arrested, jailed, medi-
cated, euthanized, or disappeared in the name of an alleged greater good? (A critical sub-theme of the 1961
Stanley Kramer film *Judgment at Nuremberg*, explored by an
American judge seeking to understand how an entire citizenry could have been unaware of horrors committed by
their elected "leader.")

The Censor works to preclude awareness. The Propagandist works to inculcate doctrine. Together they strive to
create a citizen serfdom oblivious to anything not approved by government masters. The Thief of Meaning
clinches Censor and Propagandist success by throttling a
citizenry's ability to express language needed to complain,
motivate, organize, rebel.

But like "the public," "a citizenry" is a population of
individual human persons with independent minds and,
to restate linguist McWhorter's correct observation, "The
conceptual step between a healthy person and a healthy
society is a short one." In other words, the instillation of
citizenry-scale ignorance, indoctrination, and reality denial begins with the individual.

A scene in the 1947 movie *Gentleman's Agreement*,[1]
adapted from the Laura Z. Hobson novel, characterizes
this truth. Cathy, the fiancé of the story's protagonist, tells
Phil, the protagonist's best friend, about a "horrible man"
who made bigoted remarks during a social engagement
she attended earlier that evening. When Phil, an ex-Army
captain and Jew, asks, "What did you do?" Cathy replies, "I
wanted to yell at him. I wanted to get up and leave. I
wanted to say to everyone at that table, 'Why do we sit

here and take it when he's attacking everything that we believe in? Why don't we call him on it?'" When Phil asks
again, *"What did you do?"* Cathy begins to understand not
only the nature of her guilt, but the evil her silence helped
to perpetuate.

The authoritarian-collectivist Left's war on words is a
war on the tools human beings need to accurately, consistently, and understandably express to one another the
ideas, opinions, emotions, conditions, actions, objects, and
information that make human life *human*. It is a war on
language as a means of conveying and integrating evidence, experience, perception, and reality. The toll of this
war, an up-to-the-minute body count of wounded and
meaning-deceased words, extends far beyond the examples offered. Their sum ranges from the asinine to the nation shaping, from Bill Clinton's "It depends on what the
meaning of the word *is* is" to black-robed judges "inter-
preting" what America's founders intended when they
conceived and composed *in English* our Constitution.

To glimpse the rot at the root of besmirching those
who would defend against word butchery and meaning
murder, consider the argument posited by Oliver Kamm,
author of *Accidence Will Happen: The Non-Pedantic Guide to
the English Language*.[2]

> I write a weekly language column for *The Times*
> in which I try to dispel some of the myths about
> usage. Oddly, what fascinates the pedantic imagi-
> nation is not what we can achieve with language
> but what we can proscribe. The things that stick-
> lers worry about — "decimate" in its looser sense;
> "disinterested" to mean bored rather than impar-
> tial; "none" as a plural; "they" as a gender-neutral
> singular; and many others — have nothing to do

with grammar in the sense that linguists understand the term. They're trivial complaints, at
best; more usually, they are factually wrong as-
sertions about the grammar and history of the
English language. English is not a fixed body of
rules. It does have many rules (which linguists
work out by examining the regularities of how
English speakers use their own language) and it's
possible for you, me or my newspaper to make
mistakes of syntax, semantics, spelling and punctuation. But it isn't possible for everyone, or for a
substantial body of expert users of the language,
to be wrong on the same linguistic point at the
same time. If it's widely used, it's part of the language.

   All of what I've said would be, and is, denounced by commentators who believe that defending linguistic standards, as they define them,
is crucial to social order or even civilization.

By alleging that scholars are interested in language
proscription rather than in language achievement — a
virtue neither defined nor placed in context — Kamm fails
to grasp (or grasps and denies) that achievement in every
field requires rules, definitions, and parameters, i.e., the
proscription of conflicting influences and goal-blocking ob-
stacles. While allowing that English "does have many
rules" and that it's possible for "you, me, or my newspaper
to make mistakes," he claims by implication that the
"rules" are not fixed and that he is either unwilling or unable to define even his own use of the word. His claim, "If
it's widely used, it's part of the language," can be true or
false. If "the language" is governed by rules that are not
rules, the statement is true. If his words "widely," "it," "is,"

"used," and "part" mean something different to different people, the statement is false.

Or maybe not.

And since numbers — two, four, six, eight — are no more or less crucial as concept-designators than Kamm's "decimate," "disinterested," "none," and "they" examples, this dingbat would presumably agree that two plus four equals eight if widely accepted. He might even consider the equation a linguistic achievement. Why he grants legitimacy to the rules of syntax, semantics, spelling, and punctuation is anyone's . . . gess.

The Thief of Meaning, really The *Murderer* of Meaning, is everywhere. He — and for gender-obsessed mini-minds I am not referring to maleness — was welcomed long ago into our conversations, homes, schools, and literature. He is The Censor's swindling cousin and The Propagandist's most useful ally, but he is impotent without the endorsement and participation of Consensual Conscripts, and his tool for theft and murder is also his vulnerability.

Language is its own defender. Were its professional users to stand fast as guardians of meaning and, in turn, require their readers, listeners, and viewers to rise to un-dumbed-down prose, The Murderer of Meaning would be rendered powerless.

All that is required, all that has *ever* been required, is to earnestly speak the simplest and single-most uncorruptible word in any language, the word that honorably exemplifies an unpoliticized definition of extremist, the word that makes a redundancy of modifiers like decisively, absolutely, utterly, strictly, irrevocably, unconditionally, indisputably, resolutely.

Whether for the purpose of terminating an offensive conversation — or correcting a speaker who misapplies an important word — or withdrawing children from 98,000

indoctrination camps mislabeled public "schools" — or re-
jecting news, information, and advice tailored to comple-
ment regime propaganda — or firing a politician whose
post-election actions contradict his pre-election promises
— or refusing to surrender principles in the face of opposition — or laughing in the face of pronoun redesignation
— or quitting employment at a business, institution, or
government agency that punishes independent choice and
achievement while rewarding compliance and group identity — or walking out of the office of a doctor more interested in obeying the World Health Organization and Big
Pharma than in healing — or beating to an unconscious
bloody lump (metaphorically, of course) every petty government tyrant who attempts to force a mother and father
to mutilate their confused minor child — all that is required, *all that has ever been required*, is for enough of us to
say *NO!* and by everything we hold sacred to mean what
we say.

Which has nothing to do with what "the public"
wants, thinks, feels, or votes and everything to do with
honest definitions of health, happiness, liberty, and life.

HOW NOT TO SAVE AMERICA

I n preceding chapters I have presented a decidedly American perspective, not because I am an American but because America, despite her descent into the oblivion of statist mediocrity, remains the world's bastion of hope for those who value liberty and the most stubborn obstacle in the path of those whose goal is to make of humanity one neck for one leash — or noose. For the duration of this chapter, I respectfully ask that readers keep in mind one premise and its corollary:

The principles responsible for the
creation of America are, and have always
been, required in equal measure to sustain America.
Only an independent-minded citizenry can
preserve a free independent nation.

I HAD A FRIEND, now deceased, who for twenty-seven years was a prospector in the Yukon Territory. We met in the Interior of Alaska, where he lived with his wife in a rough log cabin forty minutes by road from the nearest town. He had retired and married and settled after finding himself one afternoon shouting angrily at a passenger jet that had infringed on his privacy. In a leather pouch suspended from a strip of rawhide worn around his neck he carried a two-and-a-half-ounce gold nugget, the largest he ever found. We shared good conversations about life, philosophy, politics, grizz, gold, and his failing heart, and I spent several days collecting samples from a four-miles-distant quartz outcropping that had for years been teasing him through binoculars. Three decades later, I remember his stories and his final words to me, but most poignantly I remember his answer to my question about where to find gold.

With the certainty of a man who knows from long ex-perience the conditions required to repeat a previous achievement, my friend replied, "I can't say where you're gonna find it, but I can say where you're not gonna."

Since the principles responsible for the creation of America have always been required in equal measure to sustain America, it is not difficult to identify behaviors, ideas, actions, and policies that are *not gonna* save America. My use of the pronoun *you* in coming pages is intended to be conversational, not suggestive or accusative, although to paraphrase an American novelist and philosopher: "If the shoe fits, by all means wear it with my compliments."

Truth is not only violated by falsehood;
it may be equally outraged by silence.

Amien

The Pitiful Push

Most of us have witnessed, if not actually felt against our chests, the shove of a bully. Most of us have also probably witnessed, if not actually performed, the reactive response of shoving back — to which a bully responds by shoving again, or worse. In contemporary popular parlance, the phrase "pushing back" describes opposition to some political, legal, or moral violation that, in most instances, could have been foreseen and prevented but in all instances calls for more than an answering push. The initiation of force, whether physical or political, cannot be regarded or tolerated as a prologue to a pushing match — not if the individual, or nation, has self-respect. The response must in no uncertain terms end the force while boldly proclaiming the fate of potential future force-initiators. The concept characterized by the phrase "pushing back" must be replaced with "hitting in self-defense hard enough to end the pushing" and then, once the assault has been stopped and the assailant put down, underscored by "never again allowing a threat to become more than a threat."

Defending against the initiation of force is not a game. Pushing contests belong on elementary-school playgrounds, although even there the most effective way to deal with a bully is with a Flintstones lunchbox to the head — which was my brother's response when in the third grade he was shoved against the school wall by a bigger boy.

Make no mistake, behind every scrap of government paper that prescribes a law, regulation, ordinance, or mandate *there is a gun*. Force is government's closing argument, and it applies even to paltry so-called victimless crime and to the imposition of misdemeanor-class local codes.

Refuse to cover your face with a mask that cannot prevent alleged virus-particle transmission but that *will* deprive your brain of oxygen while trapping a stew of germs and filth against your mouth, nose, and skin — refuse to pay the fine for refusing to wear that useless, dangerous, false-security-providing symbol of compliance — refuse to be arrested and jailed for refusing to pay a fine for refusing to wear a dangerous symbol of compliance — and in the end, for abiding by reality-based independent judgment that protected you from the physical and psychological harm you were ordered to commit against yourself, out comes a gun in the hand of an unthinking government enforcer. Inside that gun, a twitchy finger-squeeze ahead of a readied firing pin, is a bullet inscribed with your name.

What is the difference between a criminal person and a criminal government? Criminal persons operate outside the bounds of law — at least prior to America's 2020 Summer of Thuggery — and in so doing risk that their behavior will be stopped and punished. Criminal governments, however, redefine the bounds of law for the purpose of legalizing their own criminal behavior and, save for citizen vigilantism, free their operatives from the risks faced by "honest" criminals.

Because the initiation of force by persons is legally proscribed, empty-handed threats of force by persons generally do not warrant preemptive forceful countermeasures. But a weapon in the hand of that person, or that person's physical capacity to inflict harm, changes everything. Likewise — and this is critical to understand — because threats of force by government are backed by the gun behind the paper authorizing the use of force, threats of force by government must be credited as the aggression they represent and countered appropriately.

The phrase "pushing back" is as feeble as the level of resistance it describes. I would be surprised if a single genuine bad actor, on the street or in a government office, doesn't regard "push-back" as both a joke and a gift, and I suspect it was a criminal who introduced the now-popular use of that pitiful concept. Righteous, earnest noncompliance requires a righteous, earnest, assertively defiant descriptor — such as *counterattack* — because the imminent initiation of force under any pretense, whether by a criminal person or a criminal government, warrants an immediate counter. And anything less than a decisive counter will result in a pushing match where the odds will ever be in the criminal rule-maker's favor.

The only pushing appropriate when confronted by force is for the exaction of damages in the aftermath of a successful counterattack, *after* the force-initiator has been put down and *after* wanna-be force-initiators have been shown that force will be met with preventative greater force.

To be successful, a counterattack must feature three fundamental characteristics: moral certainty, action willingness, and long-term prevention.

If the target of imminent initiated force is uncertain of the righteousness of his position, against a committed aggressor he lacks the strength to prevail — whether that aggressor is a risk-taking person or a protected felonious government lackey. Moral courage and the self-respect it presupposes are the most powerful causal agents in the human arsenal, which is why sophisticated criminal governments invest heavily in undermining moral certainty while culturally manipulating ethics to work in reverse.

If the target of imminent initiated force is unable or unwilling to decisively act in the service of self-defense, against a committed aggressor he lacks the strength to prevail.

And what is the point of deflecting imminent force if the manner in which it was deflected does not also discourage, if not prevent, subsequent better-armed aggression? The nature and resilience of one's enemy may well justify and require an ideological or material *coup de grâce*.

Moral persons have no obligation, and would, further, be fools, to spend their lives engaged in self-defense reruns, which is exactly the kind of life that "pushing back" guarantees.

Staying a Wrongful Course
While Knowing the Truth

In the 1958 debut episode of *The Rifleman* television series, screenplay author Sam Peckinpah dramatized a moral conundrum common to employer-employee relationships. The series' protagonist, Lucas McCain, arrives with his young son, Mark, at the New Mexico Territory town of North Fork after what they hope is the end of a long westward search for a start-over life. While checking into a North Fork hotel, Lucas, a skilled marksman, learns of a shooting match with enough prize money to help him buy the disused ranch he and Mark inspected outside of town. Early in the match, before taking his turn, Lucas is approached by the North Fork sheriff and ushered aside for a private word.[1]

"What's the matter?" Lucas asks.

"Mr. McCain," Sheriff Tomlinson begins, "I think there's something you ought to know about this town. It belongs to Jim Lewis."

"All of it?"

"Well, he tolerates me as long as I don't give him any trouble."

"Oh, I see."

"No, I'm afraid you don't. Lewis has been around here now almost four years. During that time a lot of things have happened, a lot of people have been buried. He don't lose, Mr. McCain, not ever."

"You're not volunteering this information."

"No, I'm not."

"Why don't you take off that badge," Lucas proposes, turning to leave without waiting for an answer.

The sheriff takes Lucas' arm and says, "I'll tell you why, Mr. McCain. Because as long as I wear it I can do a little good. Not much, but a little, and that's better than none at all."

Lucas breaks from the sheriff's grasp and walks back to the match.

When a man knows he is a participant in a wrongful enterprise, is doing "a little good" better than doing "none at all"? Or does such a theory help to make the wrongful enterprise possible? Is the oft-repeated defensive explanation, "If I don't someone else will," a statement of honorable intent? Or an abdication of responsibility?

When a good man learns that he has chosen a career with an enterprise fundamentally doing wrong, what are his choices if he is to remain a good man?

Consider the question in the first person as an employee of the FBI, CIA, or Secret Service. If you know that those for whom and with whom you work are betraying the Constitution they and you are employed to honor and defend — not occasionally and accidentally but routinely and willfully — is remaining in your job hoping to "do a little good" an act of moral fortitude? Or of betrayal?

If in your optimistically patriotic youth you dreamed of protecting the life of "the leader of the free world" only to discover as a Secret Service agent that the president you are assigned to protect is destroying the Constitution he and you swore to honor and defend — would you remain at your post? Would you continue to assure the safety of a man determined to eradicate the liberty and life of your countrymen, friends, and family? Would you resign in the name of preserving your moral integrity?

Or would you, in the name of moral integrity and the free-nation-defining document you swore an oath to defend against enemies foreign and domestic, act to remove this highest-possible-level enemy and destroyer?

Would you understand that there is no moral option that includes protecting a man who betrays his oath to defend your nation's Constitution? Would you understand that a government employee, *any* government employee, who chooses to "just do his job" when the job involves advancing the goals of America's enemies *is an accomplice in the destruction of America*?

The course you choose to stay is who you are.

If you work for a corporation that promotes values antithetical to your own, whether you are a manager or a janitor you are a component of what you insincerely profess to oppose. If the enterprise is also criminal, when that enterprise is exposed you will have only yourself to blame for the resulting demotion, pay cut, unemployment — or worse — that results. If you knew the truth and stayed the course you will have earned the consequence of your choice. If you did not know, you should have been paying closer attention and you will have earned the consequence of your unawareness.

Walking a path while staring at your feet can be costly. The Covid ruse offered this lesson in flashing neon.

Doctors and nurses who implemented government-, hospital-, and WHO-decreed Covid protocols in defiance of their profession's most sacred vow *personally* contributed to destroying lives and advancing a dire anti-health, anti-human, precedent-setting medical tyranny. These healthcare professionals should have known, they should have seen, they should have protested and quit.

Journalists and so-called "news" providers who brainlessly repeated the propaganda they were told to repeat, whether aware of the lies or ignorant of the truth, *personally* contributed to the damage caused by lockdowns, business closures, mask mandates, social isolation, fearmongering, shaming, "safe-and-effective" fraud, and unprecedented money-printing-caused economic inflation. These truth professionals should have known, they should have seen, they should have protested and quit.

Police officers who enforced Constitution-defiling emergency orders by fining and arresting men, women, and children with the sense to recognize nonsense and the self-respect to honor what they recognized, are *personally* responsible for defiling America's Constitution and for ruining livelihoods and lives. These professional protectors should have known, they should have seen, they should have protested and quit.

Politicians and bureaucrats who issued or failed to aggressively oppose Constitution-defiling mandates, regulations, ordinances, and rules are *personally* responsible for debauching what it means to be an American and for ruining their citizen-employers livelihoods and lives. Those who knew or suspected that Covid was not about health but about control deserve not to be unelected or fired, but handcuffed and escorted to a prison cell or gallows after, of course public trials by those whose trust they betrayed. Those who did not know, should have. Those who still do not know are too stupid to remain in positions of authority or influence.

"Just doing my job" is pure responsibility abdication.

The sheriff of the fictional town of North Fork was too much of a coward to protect the rights of the citizens who elected him, and too much of a coward to step down. He wanted to be "the sheriff;" he wanted the status and the paycheck; he wanted whatever counterfeit respect could be had. He rationalized his cowardice with the claim that doing "some" good was better than doing no good, which is only true when doing good within a system that recognizes and rewards achievement of the good.

Within a corrupt system, a system that betrays and destroys what it was created to honor and protect, those who are aware of the corruption and who choose to continue "just doing their jobs" *are the corruption*, as are those irresponsibly too unaware to see what they serve.

The Inevitable Emptiness of Teenage Activism

Adult Americans' preoccupation with implementing political "solutions" to politics-caused problems is a recipe for eventual failure. Expanding the application of political quick-fixes by "empowering" American youth with political theory is the equivalent of implementing Failure Plan B. Although the appeal of organizations like Turning Point USA and Young America's Foundation is understandable, high-school students, with perhaps a one-in-ten-thousand exception, have not acquired the cognitive maturity to meaningfully underpin political "conclusions."

Conservative political activism by sixteen-year-olds is no more durable than Leftist virtue signaling, and it is wrongfully exploitable. Teenage political "activists" lack the foundation of a developed ability to reason independently, to objectively grasp and weigh evidence and argument — virtues American education has been deliberately and successfully crafted to prevent. Such an expectation is less than premature: it is shallow initially and dogmatic ultimately, conceptually tenuous and morally dubious. Reverse engineering malleable young minds may seem a responsible expedient, but a high-school "Republican" rebuttal to Democrat propaganda pits indoctrination against indoctrination.

While the sporadically sensible Senator Ted Cruz was not entirely incorrect when he claimed that "The key to turning America around is for young people to become entrepreneurs in defense of freedom," the mold for the key must first be made. That mold, an unpoliticized system of conceptual education for the young, does not exist.

Which means: neither does the key.

Good can never lastingly prevail over evil through political action because political action is a consequence of philosophy, of what people value, of how they think, of how they were taught to think. Students who have been taught to think, to think for themselves, to reason independently, to objectively grasp and weigh evidence and argument, will as a consequence reach pro-liberty political conclusions. Then and only then will they understand and defensibly own *the source* of what they think and say — as opposed to repeating the well-intentioned ungrounded politispeak that will ultimately further statist goals.

The tenets of statism in all of its forms rest on anti-reason, anticonceptual premises. As such, these tenets can survive generations without ever having to endure logical argument. They require only repetition, mass, momentum, force, and compliance. If lasting liberty is desired, one does not fight anti-liberty politics by offering unformed minds a substitute political affiliation. One teaches unformed minds how to think conceptually and reason independently.

The rest, the best, will follow.

Justice Gone Awry at the Ballot Box

Those who have not read the Republican and Democratic Party platforms of 1856 should do so while paying particular attention to "the agitation of the slavery question," which in essence is this:

Are *all* men endowed with an inalienable right to life, liberty, and the pursuit of happiness? Or only *certain* men as determined by Democrats?

To this day, the Democratic Party's answer is the core of its class-structured social ideology and political policies. The Republican Party's answer named, in part, the following charges.

> . . . tyrannical and unconstitutional laws have
> been enacted and enforced; the right of the
> people to keep and bear arms has been in-
> fringed; the right of an accused person to a
> speedy and public trial by an impartial jury has
> been denied; the right of the people to be secure
> in their persons, houses, papers, and effects,
> against unreasonable searches and seizures, has
> been violated; they have been deprived of life,

liberty, and property without due process of law;
freedom of speech and of the press has been
abridged; the right to choose their representatives has been made of no effect; murders,
robberies, and arsons have been instigated and
encouraged, and the offenders have been allowed to go unpunished.

Does this sound familiar?

The Democratic Party's seventeen-decades-old dedication to its founding theories and logical destructive consequences is, where commitment is concerned, admirable.
But other than the authority to deny rights to certain individuals, what else did Democrats allege 168 years ago?

That it is the duty of every branch of the Government to enforce and practice the most rigid
economy in conducting our public affairs, and
that no more revenue ought to be raised than is
required to defray the necessary expenses of the
Government, and for the gradual but certain extinction of the public debt.

And:

That Congress has no power to charter a national
bank; that we believe such . . . dangerous to our
republican institutions and the liberties of the
people, and calculated to place the business of
the country within the control of a concentrated
money power, and above the laws and the will of
the people.

Does this sound *un*familiar? Does enforcing "the most
rigid economy" or ending public debt or preventing the

placement of "the business of the country within the control of a concentrated money power" even remotely re-
semble the policies of Democrats today?

Republican pundits rightly observe that Democrats
have reversed their former anti-war, anti-censorship, anti-
mega-corporation, and pro-body-autonomy positions in
favor of interventionist war, naked censorship, corporate
romance, and medical tyranny. On the surface this ap-
pears to be true. Beneath the surface, however, both parties have long employed different means to achieving the
same Big Brother end. Aside from vote-garnering lip service to traditional Party issues, there is little long-term-
results difference between Republicans and Democrats
once either gets into office. And although the degree to
which actual party goals overlap may be debatable, the deliberately misleading political-pendulum swing is not. It
travels from Right to Left and back over an ersatz spectrum averaging one presidential shift per two and a third
terms while relentlessly inching from right to *wrong* over
the human-liberty spectrum.

But . . .

The entrenchment of superficially oppositional political machines was worse than a mistake that transferred
election-outcome power from voters to party committees;
it was a seed planted to upend The Founders' system of
checks and balances by politicizing the judiciary.

No American judge, elected or appointed, whether
presiding over the highest tribunal in the land or over a
backwater municipal court, has any business attaching
political-party affiliation to his or her name. Nor has
anyone representing the protective arm of American
justice, whether the head of the DOJ or a state-police
administrator or a county sheriff or the chief of a two-cop
town.

American law is apolitical law. Once politicized, it is no longer American law.

Every justice-system candidate or employee whose name is followed by an "R" or a "D" is proclaiming that he or she will interpret, apply, and enforce the law through the lens of political affiliation — as justice-perverting and America-destroying a concept as has ever existed.

Closing One Eye and Believing with the Other

I don't know when politician wannabees realized that the way to get elected had nothing to do with moral integrity and competency and everything to do with telling "the people" what the people want to hear, but it has been so for a long, long time. And the people seldom seem to comprehend that their first response to hearing what they want should not be *yes* at the polls, but a healthy skepticism demanding answers to important questions.

What has this bromide-bullhorning person accomplished in the past? What was his relationship to government while accomplishing it? Of what does his history and résumé consist? What influences, circumstances, mentors, alliances, allegiances, and debts come with the package if the package is elected?

Is it relevant or irrelevant that as an aspiring casino kingpin private citizen Donald Trump unconstitutionally exploited eminent-domain statutes to seize and demolish private property for the construction of his casino? That his mentor had been the grotesquely hypocritical and cartoonishly corrupt political fixer Roy Cohn, chief legal counsel to Senator Joseph McCarthy during the 1950s communist witch hunt, eventually a New York Mafia-boss lawyer disbarred for attempting to force a dying client to revise his will to benefit Roy Cohn? That one term before entering the 2016 presidential race Trump was forgiven between $82 and $300 million in Trump Tower (Chicago) mezzanine-loan debt by George Soros, Fortress Investment Group, and Blackacre Capital? That his "Christianity" blossomed just in time to convince the Evangelical Right that he might be The Chosen One? That in a 2016 interview he stated unequivocally that people should use whatever bathroom "they feel is appropriate"? That his biggest campaign donor was the Israel-pandering casino billionaire Sheldon Adelson and that a pharmaceuticals giant kicked in a cool million?

Should it come as a surprise that upon becoming president he rewarded his failed-investment rescuers with magnanimous political favors and granted Adelson, described at the time by columnist Timothy Egan as "now having more influence on American foreign policy than even the Secretary of State," his wish to have the U.S. Embassy moved from Tel Aviv to Jerusalem and Neocon John Bolton appointed National Security Advisor? That during the Covid-ruse lockdowns he gave Larry Fink, globalist CEO of BlackRock, vast control over U.S. fiscal policy, a blessing that resulted in an otherwise-unachievable and often lethal transfer of wealth from private businesses to multinational mega-corporations? That while dispensing pardons to financial criminals and Israeli spies he betrayed two courageous men who exposed the government corruption *he* had promised to eradicate? That he insistently refers to the constitutional republic of America as a democracy? That his proposal to mandate a one-year jail sentence "if you do anything to desecrate the American flag" is not about defending property rights but about assigning victim status to political symbolism, as is the wont

of every dictator? That on the final day of his first administration he awarded medical malefactor Anthony Fauci a
presidential commendation? That to this day he claims to
be the "father" of a health-destroying non-vaccine and
savior of hundreds of millions of lives from a fabricated
pandemic?

This man, after campaigning on a what-the-people-
wanted-to-hear promise to rid Washington of "swamp"
creatures, promptly surrounded himself with Washington
swamp creatures only to later claim he didn't know they
were swamp creatures.

Is it possible, after a half century of eyeballs-deep immersion in billion-dollar loans, favor swapping, influence
peddling, palm greasing, reality-show posing, bankruptcy
dodging, platinum-plated shoulder rubbing, and person-
alized tutoring by a scumbag political-fixer lawyer, that
this America First pretender did not then and does not
now know the game, its players, and his part? That his
comically shallow need for an ego-affirming spotlight is
not a telling indicator of the all-about-me force that drives
him?

No, it is not possible.

And yet, hoards of good-but-gullible Americans
would rather believe what they want to hear than credit
the orator's history as relevant to probable outcome.

Question: What does "Make America Great Again" actually mean?

Answer: Whatever anyone wants "great" to mean.

Via personal subjective projection it is assumed that
the slogan's deviser intended *that* particular meaning.
Leaving aside the deviser's use of "great" to flatter whatever pleases or serves and that his devotees enthusiastically imagine strategic reasons for his speak-first-think-
later blunders — as if, preposterously, the man is playing

advanced-level chess — it is obvious that to Mr. Trump "Make America Great" means "Make America Useful."

Useful to whom?

To anyone the Trump Package owes. And if some Americans derive some short-term benefits, well, "Thanks for voting MAGA."*

Judgment is an inescapable responsibility that renders "Judge not lest ye be judged" a hypocrisy-inducer, a formula for moral abdication. The rule should be and is in reality: *Judge and expect to be judged.*

No successful business manager would hire a job candidate based on promises unsupported by a history of capability and inclination. Why do voters time and again hold their representatives in the realm of liberty-and-life protection to a lesser standard?

Believing what we want to hear when verbalized by someone who knows what we want to hear and in whom we have insufficient evidence-based reason to place our trust, is a mistake. It is a mistake befitting one fair definition of insanity: repeatedly performing an action while expecting each time a different result. A mistake certain to keep the Political Pendulum swinging until it stops where it has always been intended to stop. A mistake repeated by voters over and over and over and over and over and

---

* Trump Derangement Syndrome, or TDS, is an appellation ascribed by "the Right" to the rabidly antagonistic emotional response exhibited by "the Left" to all things Trump. Its counterpart, no less real and vision restricting, is Trump Delusion Syndrome, the rabid adoration exhibited by Trump-devotee mobs. The Trump-deranged want an America that is not America; their wish looms on a near horizon. The Trump-deluded want America to be more or less America but their MAGA-cap brims obscure the same totalitarian horizon and its alternate access route. TDS in either form is a wedge driven into America for the purpose of dividing and controlling, and then ending, America.

The Bet

To win your trust all we require
Is knowledge of your hearts' desire.
To make of you a mob we plant
A slogan you and yours will chant.

To rule this mob, to make it cheer,
We tell it what it wants to hear.
But in the end, come rise or fall,
The mob and you will face the wall.

It matters not what mob we made,
Or what you thought was our crusade.
Not Left or Right, not right or wrong,
Not bad or good, not weak or strong.

What matters all is what we get
From either side on which we bet.
And since both sides we keep in hand,
We bet you'll never understand.

From *Confessions of a Soviet Propagandist*

The Answer to Leftist News

The answer to Leftist news is not Conservative news, but objective news. The job of a reporter, whether on a battle-field or city sidewalk or in the halls of congress, is to be the eyes and ears of those who want to know what is happening where they cannot physically be. The job of the face or voice relaying to an audience what a reporter witnessed is to relay *what the reporter witnessed.*

What an event means is for individual minds — and apparently for a booming industry of surrogate thinkers known as "show hosts" — to determine and evaluate in context. Honest messengers who respect their audiences will, even when facts contradict their (or their paycheck-writer's) preferred positions, uphold the journalistic imperative of responsibly maintaining an unbroken chain of objectivity.

Clearly, Leftist news is subjective news. But if one understands that "the news" is simply a formal presentment of potentially enlightening, interesting, useful information, one also understands that any attempt to counter, color, or "balance" one variety of bias with another variety of bias makes of the message and messenger, propaganda and propagandist.

(This standard of impartiality precludes sensationalizing messages with fancy graphics and catchy music *á la* the quasi-fictional 1997 film, *Wag the Dog.*)

The answer to controlled information is liberated information offered without prejudice, selective omission, meaning manipulation, context revision, adjectival overtones, political bent, hype, slant, or filter so that its recipients can judge for themselves the information's validity and relevance to their lives.

Breathing Life into Mistakes of the Past

Lawmakers rarely correct legislative blunders by rescinding bad laws. Rather, they pass new laws intended to make bad laws "work." When the new laws fail to fix older bad laws, lawmakers pass more new laws to fix the fixes, eternally expanding a bloated cobbled-together mess.

So it is with America's historic policy blunders which, when objectively reviewed, reveal not a series of unrelated mistakes, but an orchestrated liberty-destroying program. From the mid-1800s crafting of a two-party political occupancy to the early-1900s imposition of central banking, and from forcing individuals into a Socialist retirement scheme in the 1930s and off of value-based money forty years later, American politicians relentlessly fortify their predecessors' America-destroying blunders of the past.

The anticonstitutional subgovernment in America — the "deep" or administrative state — is the penultimate result of politically creating a self-fortifying blunder.

Starting with her first extra-constitutional regulatory agency, America's internal enemies have been establishing Treason Cells that, like a cancer, grow while killing their host. In a problem-reaction-solution *modus operandi* David Icke has been astutely applying since the 1990s, authoritarian governments expand their power by adding agency after agency in response to "problems" manufactured by government.

While there are honest and well-meaning individuals in these agencies, the longer the agencies remain in existence the more corrupt they become. Why? Because these agencies were created *for that purpose* under the pretense of protecting Americans from whatever problem was invented to justify the invention of the agency.

The sole function of a moral government is *protector of individual rights*. Such a government is a guardian of liberty authorized to employ force only against those who initiate force. The only legitimate force-wielding government agents are, therefore, police to *defend* against domestic aggression, soldiers to *defend* against foreign aggression, and judges to apply objective law in cases of rights transgressions, dispute resolution, fraud, breach of contract, and *unconstitutional government initiation of force.*

Unlike individual men and women who possess singular free will, however, the ICC, FCC, EPA, FBI, CIA, USDA, DHS, IRS, DEA, DOE, DOJ, FDA, CDC and every future acronym-able agency blooming in the tiny minds of power-lusting politicians, Treason Cells are by design corruptible and free-nation destroying.

(Lord Acton's "Power tends to corrupt and absolute power corrupts absolutely" is only true if the person with power is corruptible. The assumption that all men are corruptible is a lie popularized by corrupt men attempting to excuse their own corruption, in turn given credence by the farcical myth that human beings are *born* guilty.)

Politically implanted tumors cannot be made benign in an effort to save the organism of America. They must be removed and their reestablishment forever prevented. *If* the existence of one or two such agencies can be perfectly constitutionally justified *to protect the inalienable rights of Americans*, it or they must be directly answerable to those affected by their existence.

Notably, there is a recurring opportunity to eliminate mistakes of the past. Every time the federal government "finds" itself on the brink of shutdown due to budget "problems" — also known as reality — the answer is not to revise the budget or manipulate the numbers or increase taxes or print more money or debate stopgap solutions.

The answer is to welcome shutdown as a consequence of irresponsibility and as an opportunity to amputate dozens of gangrenous appendages and to liposuck tons of bureaucratic blubber — in contrast to the Heritage Foundation's *Mandate for Leadership 2025*, written to help "the next conservative President" shed a few ounces.[2]

"The bad news," this elephantine handbook's gaggle of authors declare, "is that our political establishment and cultural elite have once again driven America toward decline." Wrong. The political establishment and "elite" are incapable of *driving* anything. Americans indoctrinated to trust political "solutions" to problems not politically solvable have merely acquiesced to authoritarian's nudge.

"The good news is that we know the way out even though the challenges today are not what they were in the 1970s. Conservatives should be confident that we can rescue our kids, reclaim our culture, revive our economy, and defeat the anti-American Left — at home and abroad. We did it before and will do it again."

Predictably, *nothing* that proceeds from this placating boast suggests knowledge of an "out." There is scarcely a recommendation that does not breathe life into mistakes of the past, condemn independent thinking to the scrapbook of history, further entrench cultural nihilism, and betray *right* by compromising with *wrong* — the contemporary understanding of which is "being pragmatic."

Mockingly, "We did it before and will do it again" is etched into the base of the Political Pendulum.

America's Second Declaration of Independence will necessitate a declaration of national bankruptcy — a condition long ago achieved and outrageously denied via deferment — so that every past self-destructive mistake can be scraped, chiseled, and swept into the trash until all that remains is America's taken-for-granted clean foundation.

No Business Like SHOW Business

Pulsing S-O-S audio accompanies a detonation fuse
burning left to right across a black screen
overlain with expanding yellow captions.

HARD HITTING

TRUTH TELLING

OFTEN EXPLOSIVE

ON YOUR SIDE

The Tom Jefferson Show!

Lights come up to a man seated outdoors
behind a microphone at a table with a blue mug
printed TOMMYJ.COM/STORE, a cow bell, and a silver whistle
framed by a red border and winking translucent stars.

"Good morning!" the man exclaims. "And welcome to this
Friday edition of The Tom Jefferson Show! I'm your host,
Sam Adams, sitting in for Thomas while he and his wife
enjoy a well-deserved extended weekend in New Orleans,

after which on his way back to Monticello he'll kick off the ninth Vote Stars and Stripes to Keep Your Rights rally at Hilton Head's Grand Casino and Convention Center. As always, the monarchy is up to no good and we have lots to cover, so stay tuned for the most insightful news analysis you've heard since this time yesterday morning."

Host reaches off camera.
Displays a 1950s Gumby claymation figure.

"Gums, who's our guest today?"

Gumby faces host. Host faces audience.

"This is Gums. I learned from Thomas that all successful political-show hosts have a special someone in the background with whom they can engage in fatuous banter."

Host looks at Gumby. Listens.

"Who? Good!"

Host places Gumby off camera. Faces audience.

"We'll be joined in the final hour of today's show by Aaron Burr to discuss the ethical pros and cons of U.S. congresspersons engaging in pistol duels, which Gums and I agree is a damn sensible idea. So . . . don't go away. We'll be back after six minutes of product sales pitches by . . ."

THE RUINATION OF AMERICA is not show business. It is not appropriate to run bedding, office-chair, joint-pain and tax-debt-relief, time-share-annulment, and dog-itch-cure promotions every ten or twelve minutes to stretch an hour of current-event commentary into three hours of chat theater, and it sure as hell is not appropriate for media personalities to amass wealth while perched atop the stooped shoulders of a collapsing nation.

Question: Why would anyone seeking information not constrained by FCC regulations and corporate-agenda parameters expect to receive such information from a guy sitting behind a neon-illuminated battleship-size desk surrounded by walls of video-effect distractions punctuated by pop-music excerpts and dark symphonic overtures? Or from "Deep in the bowels of an underground whatever under a towering nondescript whatever where our leader is taking a bite to the radical Left and putrid Swamp"?

Answer: Because we have been programmed to accept and ingest what is conveniently available, processed for consumption, trendily packaged with the coolest bells and whistles — and to accept as *normal* an inescapable cacophony of cognition-desensitizing noise and queasy-cam visuals at home, work, the pub, the laundromat, the airport, the gas pump.

That audiences have been conditioned to need flash-and-dash spectacle with *everything* is a culture- and mind-destroying phenomenon. Playing to and falling for this consciousness-insulting foolishness dilutes the value of the subject and perpetuates numbskull creation. If the subject or message is unable to attract and hold an audience, assuming it is accurately and articulately presented, adding pageantry and calling it a "show" will not elevate the subject or advance the message.

Am I suggesting that talk-show hosts have nothing to say worth hearing? No. Some are intelligent, aware, literate, and earnest while giving voice to the prerequisite for the possibility of action and the primary ingredient for realistic hope: truthful information. But with few exceptions they share message-degrading characteristics certain to exempt meaningful action and to permanently relegate hope to the domain of the unrequited. In other words, too many are charismatic celebrities exploiting a demand-driven entertainment-market niche, even though they believe they are "helping the cause by spreading the word."

Unhelpfully, the most popular among them have blind spots wide enough to accommodate the passage of an infantry division. Not only are they nearsighted when connecting current events to causal history and globalist motives, they skillfully navigate parameters set by their overseers — the Federal Communications Commission, broadcast-station managers, salary-paying sponsors, and audience numbers — without whose approval their popularity would be curtailed. The brightest among them occasionally rebroadcast unfiltered information borrowed from original thinkers who have for decades been describing what America and the world face today, but to the edge of the bigger truth is as close as they have the vision and courage to come.

Which is to say that they exemplify the old German adage, "Whose bread I eat is whose song I sing."

(Show hosts allowed on FCC-regulated corporate-sponsor-dependent radio and television are allowed because they pose no serious threat to the forces aligned against America. The hangers-on at Fox, for example, will ever be overpaid bread eaters.)

Although it is profoundly just to laugh at willful insanity — petty tyrants seeking to feed their empty souls by controlling others deserve to be lavished with the public ridicule they fear — the artfully humorous Chris Plante shares with his fellow showmen most of their blind spots. And while Plante achieves theoretical good by joking from a popularity-protected podium, practical good can only be achieved when enough people laugh openly and unapologetically not in the privacy of their living rooms, but in the faces of petty tyrants.

"The most banned network in the world," presciently named Infowars years before the information war would be recognized for what it is, subverts its message by resorting to sensationalism. While Alex Jones' self-sustaining financial model is worthy of emulation, *his* emulation of corporate-media show-boating is message diminishing. Jones' oft-mocked "conspiracy theory" warnings and predictions have consistently proven accurate, but his message would be more widely respectfully regarded if he would stop adulterating it with focus-perturbing slick visual hullabaloo.

Am I suggesting that it is not a relief to hear voices confidently putting into words what is right and true about forces gathered against America? Of course not. But no matter how often or enthusiastically those voices assure their audience that their particular message is critical to the future of America, if it sounds like entertainment, looks like entertainment, tastes, feels, smells and sells like entertainment, it's entertainment.

And most minds will subconsciously file the product under "Entertainment."

The most prominent descendants of the late Rush "Doctor of Democracy" Limbaugh are to the ideological battle for America what pro boxing and the UFC are to personal and national self-defense. Strip away the packaging, rules, stopwatches, product banners, bikini'd bimbos strutting with round cards, station breaks, and killer soundtrack, what remains is an announcer describing to show attendees two opponents in a mutually consensual fisticuffs contest vying for a trophy.

Which is fine . . . for entertainment.

But what if one of these opponents happens to be an honest man attending to the business of his life only to innocently become the victim of force initiated by an assailant with above-the-law protection? Would packaging for commercial consumption this man's fight for his life be an act of respect?

America entered the death-throes stage of collapse long ago. An unprecedented life-furthering idea has for more than a century been fighting to survive — not in The Octagon but in reality against thieves, rapists, and murderers with above-the-law protection. The men, women, and children America was created to protect from the initiation of force are being forced to their knees by their sworn protectors while talk-show stars package their life-or-death struggle with only slightly less festoonery than television sports coverage.

Were Samuel Adams, George Washington, Richard Henry Lee, or Thomas Jefferson alive, do you suppose they would be hosting the "The Sam Adams Hour"? "Under the Cherry Tree with George"? "Life, Liberty, and Lee"? Or "The Tommy J Show"? Do you suppose they would be interrupting every few minutes their life-or-death message so that Adams can tout his dog's favorite nutritional supplement? Or so that Washington can shill for an ax-sharpening service? Or so that Lee can plug his latest ghost-written book while Jefferson reminds us of his chronic back pain?

Presenting any crucial subject on a par with anti-aging cream and Hair Club for Men commercials makes a burlesque of the subject and a fool of the presenter. The ideas that gave birth to America and the ideas that are destroying America are not entertainment. They are not for "shows." They are not vehicles for product pitches or follower-collectors or financial enrichment or ratings enhancement.

They are a matter of life and death.

Question: What if the reason Leftists seem unable to successfully host political "shows" is not, as Conservative show hosts have suggested, because Leftists lack wit, humor, and personality? What if it's not even because, when broadcast, Leftist ideology sounds as bad as it is? What if the *real* reason is that Leftists are too earnestly, too busily, and too successfully crafting in their image the mound of excrement they have long envisioned for America?

Answer: Three months after this chapter was posted as a video, Vladimir Putin asked Tucker Carlson: "Are we having a talk show or a serious discussion?"

Investing in The Label Factory

Each of us is a product of life-spanning influences: from how we were raised, mentored, and educated while coping with early environmental challenges — to how we negotiated maturing desire and ambition — to how we manage the consequences of our adult choices and actions. Certainly we can be described, by others or ourselves, as happy or morose, passive or aggressive, boisterous or demure, athletic, self-motivated, conscientious, lazy, reliable, old-fashioned, shy, hypocritical, dark-skinned or light, tall or short, young or old, blond or brunette, male or female. Such descriptors are to our families, friends, associates, and selves communicable evaluations of how we look and behave, a reduction-to-words of who we outwardly seem to be, a linguistic effort at giving human substance to our monikers. Whether accurate, fair, realistic, or otherwise, such terms are used to describe a portrait of personal characteristics in the same way an author might introduce the *dramatis personae* in a work of fiction.

They are not ID tags assigned for the purpose of sorting, separating, or segregating women and men into sociopolitical categories, although the accidental among such descriptors are prime candidates. One of the foremost strategies employed by those who want to rule is to fashion the merely descriptive into a brand with a predetermined politically useful bundle of grievances. Once officially branded, the wannabe ruler's propaganda machine goes to work disseminating the notion that what these suddenly-in-the-news groups all suddenly have in common is victimhood. Once a group, *any* group, is momentarily in the spotlight, the wannabe ruler and his toadying propagandists are ready with photo-op promises of advocacy, favor, restitution, mitigation, and opportunities for advancement — if only the group will commit its trust, money, and votes to its special-interest custodian.

The consequence of sociopolitical pigeonholing in a nation founded to protect the rights of its individual citizens — whether one is printing and selling or buying and wearing his particular brand's label — is destructive: politically to the concept of individual rights, philosophically to individual identity. There is no such thing as "group rights," and while we should be free to associate and form alliances with fellows whose interests, backgrounds, ideas, heritage, and goals we share, playing into any form of the "group power" or "group representation" game is dangerous in the long term no matter what political treats may be had in the short.

Although I am personally unable to think of myself within the brackets of ethnicity, sexual preference, religious affiliation, income spectrum, age range, or political party — and will never comply with the census-taker's request to provide such information — I am aware that there are people who seriously and primarily self-identify as black, white, brown, homosexual, heterosexual, middle-class, middle-age, Christian, Jewish, atheist, Republican, Democrat. I am equally aware that by such self-compartmentalization the individual women and men who comprise politicized groups — including those at the top reaping the greatest favor — will ever be regarded by their alleged political advocates as useful, controllable, faceless.

Right and wrong have nothing to do with numbers or affiliations. Not in reality and not in a sociopolitical system founded on the principle of inalienable rights. This is true no matter what politically profitable question inspires group formation. Every individual American's individual political representative has sworn to preserve and protect America's defining legal blueprint. Attending to and rewarding groups seeking "more" or "other" or "special" is outside these representatives' legal and moral capacity to reward and must in no uncertain terms be prevented, not given credence and sustenance.

By the same logic it is a mistake to confer, accept, or repeat inaccurate labels applied to the class of subhumanity that seeks to collectivize and control humanity. Referring to a dictator as something more than a dictator bolsters his lies and demeans whatever honorable title he wants the world to award him. And referring to wannabe controllers as "the elite," an assignation these degenerates fully believe *should* apply to their smaller-than-life, frightened, megalomaniacal selves, blesses evil with false moral recognition because there is nothing "elite" about monsters, parasites, vampires, leeches, fiends, demons, predators, destroyers.

The politicization of groups is as statist a practice as has ever been foisted on individuals. In a nation founded on the principle of sacrosanct individual rights, The Label Factory has no place.

The Pious-Pundit Pulpit

Reason is the Devil's harlot, who
can do nought but slander and harm
whatever God says and does.

Martin Luther

Question with boldness even the
existence of a God; because, if there be one,
he must more approve of the homage of
reason, than that of blindfolded fear.

Thomas Jefferson

Which will it be?

The authors of America's Constitution did not call upon or even reference God, Jesus, Christianity, or Faith when formulating their doctrine for the creation and maintenance of a free, independent, rights-respecting nation. America's founders were deists, not zealots or even religionists, and by design they separated church from State and State from church.

Christian Conservative talk-show hosts would do well to emulate this example, if necessary by referencing and applying to their work the *reason* The Founders' specified that "no religious test shall ever be required as a qualification to any office or public trust under the United States." Religion *personally respected* is no more suited to politicization and sleeve-wearing than is any other private choice. It is, however, optimally suited to collectivize-by-group and divide-to-conquer exploitation.

(These are not the words of a non-believer slighting those who earnestly strive to live according to their beliefs. So long as the moral canons of believers and non-believers prohibit the initiation of force and fraud against their fellow human beings, both can stand side by side as allies against evil.)

The references to supernatural authority in America's Declaration of Independence — "Nature's God," "endowed by their Creator," "Supreme Judge," and "with a firm reliance on the protection of divine Providence" — were in 1776 and will forever remain the necessary literal repudiation of the British Crown's claimed Divine Right of Kings. These references were not then and should not today serve as jumping-off-points for politics-affiliated religiosity, neither as justification for local faith-based ordinances or as seeds for growing a national theocracy — and not only because religious sects of every variety share an abysmal rights-defiling record of governance.

It is crucial to understand that America's Constitution neither asserts nor implies Supreme Being dominion or authority and, most conspicuously, contains no reference whatever to biblical doctrine. This is as it should be — not for the purpose of denying personally held religious values, which America's Constitution recognizes as important enough to explicitly protect, but for the purpose of cleanly distinguishing nation-defining rights from every form of extra-constitutional influence.

Pious pundits who hold the Republic of America as their political standard, even if only for America's promise to protect the free exercise of religion, will not save their republic from wickedness and self-destruction by implying that God co-authored America's founding document. Conservative Christians should leave history revision to statists and esteem two irrefutable facts as consummate moral pillars.

First, wherever individual human beings stand on the fields of politics and philosophy, it is by our actions, not our exhortations, that we announce to the world who we are. And second, whatever we hold as true, whether derived from this world or from "the next," the principles responsible for the creation of America are required in equal measure to sustain America.

Which — unless the goal of Christian Conservatives is the remaking of America according to Biblical doctrine — presupposes resisting the temptation to credit religion as responsible for the founding of America.

Easy Street

In "Gimme What You Got" from his 1989 album *The End of the Innocence*, Don Henley sings, "Here in the land of the free and the home of the brave, the first word that baby learns is *more*." While not unanimously true, we are surrounded by, if not crushed beneath, proof of the statement's general veracity. On a continuum paralleling the one occupied by *more* and *enough* rests one of the stickiest words of all.

Easy.

Only an *independence-capable* citizenry can preserve a

free independent nation. Reflexively seeking "easy" — as distinguished from *making efficient* — leads to a distancing from the workings of whatever was made easy. To the extent of that distancing, it leads to dependence.

In a moral society with honest political representation and a functioning system of justice, the price of ease and convenience up to a reasonably defined *enough* only marginally includes risk of harm resulting from system dependence. But en route to a master-and-serf dystopia — predictively portrayed in stories like *Anthem*,[3] *Nineteen Eighty-Four*, and *The Hunger Games*[4] and steadily transitioning from fiction to reality under an assortment of big-lie headlines — risk and harm are certainties exploited to achieve through fear an authoritarian "problem solving" end.

The road to such a destination, at first a wagon track, then railed, paved, and digitally warp-speeded, has been traveled predominantly without awareness and with an impulsive need for more, faster, easier. And when more, faster, and easier are offered "for free" or with no-money-down affordable monthly payments, most travelers answer, "Gimme what you got."

Although usually paraphrased and separated from its nineteenth-century context for modern application, Ben Franklin's "Those who would give up essential liberty to purchase a little temporary safety, deserve neither liberty nor safety" speaks in any century to an inevitable conclusion: that such a trade will not in the end provide liberty or safety except for the anointed Providers of Liberty and Safety because they, at any time and for any reason, can retract liberty and safety.

Likewise, those who would trade independence for convenience deserve neither. Beyond a practical tipping point, they will possess neither.

Ease-amplification and comfort-enhancement technology — innovations, for example, that enable users to solve mathematical problems with no knowledge of mathematics; or motor-vehicle frills such as remote start, self-adjusting seats/mirrors/headlights, anti-lock brakes, rain-sensing wipers, near-object detection, attractively voiced GPS guidance; or "smart" phones, devices, and cities — beckon entire societies to trade personal knowledge and functional autonomy for easier, faster, more. From relying on power, water, sewer, and trash-collection monopolies to ushering children onto yellow shuttles bound for public indoctrination centers, system dependency has become perfunctory. Whether ingesting captured-agency-okayed nutrition-depleted meats, fruits, and vegetables or swilling colored fizzy liquid sugar and lab-concocted snacks or injecting pharma-industry-incentivized regulator-approved medications or obeying the doctor's orders without understanding what the medical cartel means when demanding compliance to its "Standard of Care," Americans not only wade into a sea of ill health and drug-use habituation, but are encouraged to do so.

Every time we allow Google's free email service to automatically correct our spelling errors, we substitute what should be an ever-expanding understanding of language and expression for ignorance-perpetuating "convenience" and AI control. Every time we reduce to an acronym some meaningful phrase we are too rushed or lazy to pronounce in its entirety, we minimize concept respect and meaning. Every time we rush to buy the hottest new technological thingy — guaranteed, of course, to make life easier — we invite repercussions not mentioned on the product's precaution insert and, even if they were, most buyers would check the "I agree to these terms" box without reading the terms.

I am not belittling innovations that make life's tasks more efficient and less wearing. I appreciate that my chainsaws have cushioned grips, that my bedside clock features an alarm function, that my pants have pockets, that my well water is delivered with an electric pump so I don't have to carry buckets from the creek, that my word processor enables me to rearrange ideas without having to retype everything, that the transmission in my truck is synchromeshed so I don't have to double clutch. And I am not saying that *my* definition of enough, which derives from my preference to keep a close and knowing relationship with the tools of life, should be everyone's.

But I *am* saying that only an independence-capable citizenry can preserve a free independent nation, and that those who would trade independence for convenience will, in the end, achieve neither.

The creation of America was decidedly *in*convenient for those who made her creation possible. The convenience trap is a more powerful weapon against the sustaining of America than any enemy-fired munition ever developed. And what comes next to ease the discomfort of thought and conscious effort?

Palm-implanted XtrasmartPhones™ featuring heart-rate, blood-pressure, stress-level, and current-mood forwarding to government-assigned physicians and psychiatrists? Or quarterly vaccine-passport reminders with shock punishment for missed screenings and Central Bank Digital Currency-account suspension for missed boosters? Or light-speed data streaming so that on-the-go implantees can enjoy feature films and electronic "books" in under a minute? Or grammar-enhancement software that makes text messages and emails read as if composed by the latest trending author? Or an always-on Selfie Cam linked to the trending YouTube channel, "My Life in Real Time"? Or innovative apps like Vote by Phone, Date by Phone, Educate and Graduate by Phone, Raise Your Kids by Phone, Diet by Phone, and How to Survive Waiting for Your Upgraded Phone? Or phone-bill rebates for maintaining a Class A social-credit score? Or an AI-robot-to-human ratio sufficient to render half of humanity "useless"?

Imagine life never again inconvenienced by the burden of authentic human-to-human communication. By the encumbrances of genuine friendship. By the responsibilities that come with giving thought and meaning to our words and to doing in the real world what we say we intend to do. Imagine life incrementally, glacially over decades, pried free from thought and effort, rescued from risk and responsibility, divorced from humanity.

Imagine a world without a place, a haven, a *nation* founded to protect the fundamental requirements of life as a human being.

America will never be saved, which means *restored to what she was created to be*, by a citizenry of convenience-reliant, comfort-obsessed automatons. Easy Street is every day making the subjugation of Americans a cakewalk.

Facebook Fools and YouTube Yellowbellies

Censorship is the supreme enemy of liberty. Those who lend their names to the industrial-scale implementation of censorship are as responsible for the destruction of liberty as are the minions paid to silence free speech. If only one in four of seventy-five million American-election-fraud victims had in early 2021 rejected and abandoned Facebook, YouTube, and Twitter in recognition of the evil of censorship, those seventeen or eighteen million ripples would have become a tidal wave of opposition solidarity.

(The question of legally prohibiting private organizations from engaging in censorship is easily answered by defining *ownership*. What a newspaper proprietor prints in *his* newspaper is for him to decide. Ownership where the aforementioned social billboards are concerned, however, is clouded not only by these billboards' government ties (congressional show-hearings notwithstanding) but by government involvement in the creation of these billboards and their means of broadcast. There is abundant evidence to reasonably affirm that they did not arise from nerd-in-a-garage free-enterprise startups, but from taxpayer expropriations channeled through federal agencies, which entirely disintegrates the "private" argument.)

Leaving aside warnings by former Google and Facebook executives of the vulnerability-targeting, dopamine-hit-craving, and mind-hacking schemes knowingly built into social-media platforms that are, according to these insiders, "ripping apart the fabric of society,"[5] and leaving aside the former little-birdie perch acquired by the non-genius controlled-opposition corporate front-man Elon Musk, anyone who contributes to censorship-practicing media is supporting the practice of censorship. That tens of millions of pro-America voters are too lazy or busy or short-sighted or convenience-obsessed or unaware to recognize such an unsubtle self-preservation premise speaks volumes about America's likely future.

Conspicuous "pro-America" broadcasters such as Dan Bongino, Tucker Carlson, Mark Levin, Charlie Kirk, Dana Loesch, Candace Owens, Chris Plante, and Dennis Prager patronizing Facebook equals Bongino, Carlson, Levin, Kirk, Loesch, Owens, Plante, and Prager giving the rabidly anti-America super-censor Zuckerberg their professional and personal okay. These broadcasters are not fighting censorship by avoiding its redacting razor, they are giving their power to that razor. They are not fighting censorship by turning censorship against itself — which may or may not be what they think they are doing — they are assuring an anti-America censorship monster that they are morally myopic or intellectually dishonest and *absolutely not serious* when railing against censorship.

Every time Bongino reminds his audience that he will never "BS" them, which he does repeatedly, until he removes his name from Facebook he is BS-ing his audience. Time will tell what Carlson chooses when Musk's what-they-want-to-hear mask can no longer hide the what-he-makes-and-why visage underneath.

What's the matter, boys and girls? Do your besties live on Facebook and Instagram? Does Sue Wojcicki send you a portion of the money your YouTube channel makes for her? Have you not yet personally been censored?

Are you afraid that if you tell your followers you will no longer donate to the censors' bank that your followers won't follow you elsewhere? That they lack the intellectual and moral fortitude it took you too long to find? That they, like the dufus duo in the closing scene of Peter Weir's masterful *The Truman Show*, might respond to your departure from Silicon Valley's rendition of Truman's manipulated world by saying, "Let's see what else is on"?

Evil adores weaklings and hypocrites. It cannot survive without them.

Acquiescing to the Essentially Anti-American

The Covid ruse was the most out-in-the-open power-grab event in a long series of power-grab events, but it was also an unprecedented "What can we get away with?" test. Not only was horrific medical tyranny sweepingly imposed, but an entirely new concept of personal value was smugly injected into the American psyche under the headings "essential" and "nonessential."

In a free nation, producers and consumers define which economic endeavors are essential and which are not — in good times and in bad.

If, for example, *you* own a bakery and are willing to conduct business while under assault — whether by foreign bombs, domestic thugs, or a government-declared health emergency — the choice is *yours*. If your employees want to work and your suppliers want to deliver, the choice is *theirs*. If your customers want to buy your bread and pastries — whether while sharing conversation at the counter or meeting in the basement wearing biohazard suits — the choice is *theirs*.

As is any risk.

Authoritarian apparatchiks have no more right to force you out of a relationship than you have to force your workers, suppliers, and customers into one. Not for a year, not for two weeks to "flatten the curve," not for a day. Their Faucis, Birxes, comically uniformed surgeons general, and WHO supplicants are welcome to voice and defend recommendations in public debate with experts not sucking from straws in the taxpayer-filled government trough. They are welcome to suggest and welcome to ask, but anything more aggressive warrants self-defense.

In a free nation there is only one legitimate question regarding the "essential" nature of a business, and only the owner of that business has the right to provide an answer.

Is my business essential to me?

Subsequent questions are the private concern of those who work for, supply, or buy from the owner of that business.

Power-lusting politicians and viruses are fraternal twins. Both are oblivious to moral right and wrong, advancing wherever possible on weakness and vulnerability until stopped by superior force. Both have a common ally: their victims' inability or unwillingness to resist. Both have a common enemy: biological antibodies for one, moral-intellectual antibodies for the other.

In the same way that bad food combines with physical and mental sloth to become primers for disease vulnerability, the assumption that government permission is required for free men and women to do as they please with what they own is a primer for enslavement. Entrepreneurs no longer even think to question, never mind challenge, the permits, licenses, certificates, and inspections — the what, where, when, how, and with-whom controls enforced by fines, revocations, and closures — that proclaim beyond doubt that ownership and property rights are fiction.

What once would have been regarded as a pocket-lining protection racket — "do what I say or me boys'll shut ya down" — and met with indignant laughter and a tar-and-feathers party is today an uncontroversial pocket-lining protection racket given the force of law under the uncontroversial magical "For the public good."

Having failed to confidently defend the meaning of ownership, having sacrificed their right to freely engage in trade by trading their rights piecemeal for bureaucratic permissions, it was but a minor step for business owners to submit to the pronouncement that some businesses are essential while others are not.

In a free nation, in good times and in bad, every business is essential to someone. In a free nation facing bad times, petty tyrants, whether skulking in city halls or state capitals or the White House, are the human equivalent of viruses and the ultimate nonessentials. Their whining "for the public welfare" platitudes, as if men and women mature enough to own property and engage in business are helpless children, presage freedom's end.

The Covid lockdowns were never about health. They were about controlling human life and reshaping economies through destruction. They were also a test, but not only for the tyrants who declared them and the armed minions who enforced them. It would have been a glorious save-America moment had American businessmen and women boldly reclaimed rights incrementally relinquished by refusing to accept the "nonessential" labels pasted across their foreheads by their wannabe masters.

The vision, commitment, and courage it takes to create a business is required in equal measure to sustain that business. It is the personal-scale manifestation of what America was founded to represent and protect. And what is true for business creation is true for every level of productive human effort, for *your* productive effort — whatever form it may take. Your work, whether a long-planned career or a soul-deep calling or a pay-the-bills expedient, represents your ability to live as an independent person.

It is *yours*. It is *essential*.

No one has the right to tell us otherwise, to nudge us into dependency, to redefine us as Wards of The State, to enlist us as destroyers of America under the fear- and guilt-motivated pretense of saving America. Tyrants have only the power we grant them by acquiescing, by giving in, by failing to understand that the guard on the bridge between liberty and enslavement is self-respect, by failing to answer the initiation of force with the one word that honorably exemplifies an unpoliticized definition of extremist, the answer that even domesticated animals will give when threatened.

Revolution is saying NO! en masse
after too many for too long
failed to say NO! as individuals.

A Gentleman's Wager

"How Not to Save America" means "How Not to Save the
World," because the unique constitutional republic created by The Founders achieved a bulwark against totalitarianism that shone even in the world's darkest corners
as an example of what is possible, which is why statists at
home and globalists everywhere consider America the
ultimate enemy and final obstacle in their quest for a
planet-wide master-and-serf society.

The pushing game, moral cowardice, kiddie activism,
disparaging politicized justice while empowering its party-
affiliated arbiters and enforcers, trusting empty promises,
Conservative journalism, bolstering past failures, framing
news and ideology as entertainment, convenience addiction, group self-identification, American-theocracy court-
ing, whining about censorship while sharpening its razor,
trading self-respect for self-destruction — are part of a vo-
luminous list of problem-reactions that, where America's
restoration is concerned, will prove impotent.

Where I to add a fourteenth I would title it "Ripples
Outward from the Self," because before one has any business working to restore a nation, one's own house must be
in order. By contrast, working to destroy a nation requires
no such moral rectitude. One can lie, cheat, steal, abuse,
manipulate and control, seek and accept the unearned,

preach one code while living by another, and make a perfectly effective destroyer. Where America's destruction is concerned, hypocrisy and corruption are meritorious in the statist's playbook. When combined with patient internal subversion they produce what Yuri Bezmenov disclosed after his defection from the Soviet Union:[6]

> ... most of these nasty things are done to America by Americans with the ideological help of the Communist subverters. Most of the actions are overt, legitimate, and easily identifiable. The only trouble is they are "stretched in time." In other words, the process of subversion is such a long-term process that an average individual, due to the short time span of his historical memory, is unable to perceive the process of subversion as a consistent and willful effort.
>
> America is obviously a stronger force that Communism is unable to defeat. But it is possible to conquer this nation using the preconditions I have described, created by Americans themselves, and diverting America's attention away from these mortally dangerous preconditions.

Beyond the manner in which I have consciously lived from the moment I realized in 1982 what it meant to be an American and America's likely future, that future is out of my hands. But in defense of these "How Not to Save America" observations, I offer a gentleman's wager.

If by 2044 America has been restored by means of the techniques I have just disparaged, I will eat the hat I designed in response to "Make America Great Again" and erect a monument to being wrong. Of course, whether

America has by then been deleted from Neuralinked AI-cloud history or is merely two decades farther down the road over which it has been coasting for two centuries, the push-backers, just-doing-my-job halfwits, child activists, promise believers, label wearers, preacher pundits, censorship hypocrites, and self-respect erasers will have been silenced; I will be unavailable to say "I tried to tell you" even if such was my inclination; and statists will have won the hell on earth they so richly deserve.

I would like to be wrong. I would rather eat a perfectly good hat and erect a monument to apology than witness the postponed funeral of a nation *given at her birth* the means to remain healthy, but I am not wrong and it will not take twenty years to prove it.

3

TAKING JUSTICE BACK
FROM DEAD HANDS: A RECKONING

*The question is nothing less, than whether the most
essential rights of personal liberty shall be surrendered,
and despotism embraced in its worst form.*

Daniel Webster

W hen ordinary citizens see that they have
placed justice in a dead hand, they must take
justice back into their own hands where it was
once at the beginning of all things. The affirmation of this
principle is not a defiance of the law, but the fundamental
assertion of it by self-governing men. When a "supreme
Law of the Land" is framed upon the blood-baptized
bedrock of a Declaration that named and sanctified for the
first time in history *the individual person's inalienable right to
life and liberty*, no judicial interpretation may, for any reason excepting as an individual infringed another's rights,
alienate a person from life or liberty.

Although every rights violation by government is an

abomination, a government that violates the *fundamental* right, the right to life, is criminal beyond forgiveness or redemption. Which is to say, since government is not an unthinking amoral force of nature but a composite of adult men and women with distinct identities responsible for making adult choices, any person in government who chooses to enact, support, enforce, or facilitate any law or administrative regulation that violates this fundamental right is *personally guilty of committing against an innocent victim the consequence that results.*

Military conscription, known benignly in America as "selective service" and "the draft," constitutes a crime beyond forgiveness or redemption. When the exalted black-robed guardians of America's Constitution unanimously determined in 1918 that coerced military servitude is *not* an abrogation of inalienable rights and that the supreme law of our land *authorizes* government cancellation of the fundamental right, Owen Wister's 1902 description of justice placed in dead hands became positively charitable.

The hands of an entire U.S. Supreme Court proved to be not dead, but evil, as were and are the hands of every concurring jurist since.

To an Imbecile Senator and a Hollywood Hobbit

Twenty years ago, in response to the stated position of a Montana senator and a series of radio ads, I composed and distributed a pamphlet titled, "Life, Liberty, and Selective Service: A message for thinking American males aged 17 - 26." Over the next year I handed copies to high-school students while once a week inserting ten or twenty at a time in the Selective Service-brochure holder displayed

on post-office counters. As I began the outline for this
chapter I recalled that somewhere in a box of files lay my
one remaining copy of that pamphlet. I found it, read it,
and, realizing I was about to write the same words in refu-
tation of a horrendous injustice never made right, include
it here.

SEPTEMBER 2004: Conservative talk radio is currently
host to a barrage of ads reminding 18-year-old boys to
register with Selective Service. The campaign refers to its
target audience as "men" but is clearly not intended to appeal to a man's reasoning mind. One painfully long install-
ment describes registration as an attribute of manhood
compared to breaking inanimate objects with one's head.
Another features lovable *Lord of the Rings* movie star Sean
Astin, trustworthy defender of the good against computer-
generated evil, extolling the ease of registration and trumpeting the terrific government opportunities forfeited by
boys who neglect to register. A third warns more-mindful
youths that registration is "the law."

Draft-reinstatement discussions make the news from
time to time as idle speculation by open-minded politicians. Montana Senator Conrad Burns, diffidently poised
straddling a well-defined fence, blends seamlessly. According to Burns spokesman J.P. Donovan, the senator hasn't
"made up his mind on the draft" but believes "national
service is good for young people."

How can any thinking American adult, let alone a federal lawmaker, be undecided on military conscription?

Whether reinstatement looms on the horizon or this
do-your-duty propaganda is a just-in-case contingency,
someone in Washington anticipates a shortage of U.S. military personnel. With enlistments up after 9/11, with flags
flying high and soldier songs topping the Country charts,

what conditions hint at an insufficient volunteer soldiery?

A free man's desire to enlist in his free nation's military comes from knowing *why* he should fight. Does the current administration believe that the next generation of draft-age boys may actually question the validity of risking their lives in a war with flip-flopping objectives? Or that draft-age boys see draft-age boys dying unnecessarily in official-policy asymmetrical warfare? Or that President Bush's proud boast of Americans' ability to "sacrifice for the liberty of strangers" was understood too well by too many parents of draft-age boys?

So long as Americans value life and liberty, there will be no shortage of volunteers in the face of a demonstrable threat to life and liberty. Someone in Washington, however, intends to be ready to force American boys into a war incapable of inspiring volunteers.

Nothing defines "involuntary servitude" more eloquently than military conscription. No matter what the Supreme Court has to say, it is unconstitutional. Even without Amendment XIII, the Bill of Rights guarantees that "The enumeration in the Constitution of certain rights shall not be construed to deny or disparage others retained by the people" — the foremost of which *and guarantor of all others* is the right to life. And there is obviously no comparison between the quality of a volunteer army and a conscripted one. But legal and practical arguments are postscripts to the moral one: that the draft utterly negates a man's right to his own life, that his life belongs to The State, and that The State may claim his life by ordering its sacrifice in whatever war it decrees.

A government that abrogates its citizens' right to life is asserting that no other rights are possible, which is true. If hobbit Astin had been hired to squeakily read an honest ad, it might go something like:

"This message is for American boys nearing the age of 18. Under penalty of law you must register with Selective Service in the event that the U.S. government deems it necessary to force you into military internment. It is not for you to choose to risk death or disfigurement in combat against a nation you may or may not perceive to be a threat to your life and liberty, because both are the property of a government qualified to make such judgments on your behalf and to dispose of your life accordingly.

"But there's good news. When you register you become eligible for employment with the government and to borrow some of the money taken from your parents in taxes, unless of course you are drafted and killed in battle."

Might such an ad read by a Hollywood hobbit help the irresolute senator formulate an opinion?

A Constitution Libeled

On 9 December 1814, U.S. Senator Daniel Webster delivered to the House of Representatives his insensed opposition to President Madison's proposal for national military conscription in support of what would become known as the War of 1812. Senator Webster said, in part:[1]

> Is this, sir, consistent with the character of a free
> government? Is this civil liberty? Is this the real
> character of our Constitution? No, sir, indeed it is
> not. The Constitution is libeled, foully libeled.
> The people of this country have not established
> for themselves such a fabric of despotism. They
> have not purchased at a vast expense of their
> own treasure and their own blood a Magna Carta

to be slaves. Where is it written in the
Constitution, in what article or section is it
contained, that you may take children from their
parents, and parents from their children, and to
compel them to fight the battles of any war in
which the folly or the wickedness of government
may engage it? Under what concealment has this
power lain hidden which now for the first time
comes forth, with a tremendous and baleful
aspect, to trample down and destroy the dearest
right of personal liberty?

One hundred and four years later, after coerced military servitude was enacted as law by Congress upon entering World War I, the U.S. Supreme Court unanimously
upheld the "Selective Draft" as constitutional. Chief Justice
Edward White wrote:[2]

Thus, sanctioned as is the act before us by the
text of the Constitution and by its significance as
read in the light of the fundamental principles
with which the subject is concerned, by the
power recognized and carried into effect in
many civilized countries, by the authority and
practice of the colonies before the Revolution, of
the States under the Confederation, and of the
Government since the formation of the
Constitution, the want of merit in the conten-
tions that the act in the particulars which we
have been previously called upon to consider
was beyond the constitutional power of Congress
is manifest.

One must conclude that White's collaborating fellow

bench-sitters were comparably illiterate and ignorant, but, where "interpretation" of America's Constitution is concerned, illiteracy and ignorance have since proved congenital, perhaps viral. Although Senator Webster's further challenge, "Who will show me any Constitutional injunction which makes it the duty of the American people to surrender everything valuable to life, and even life itself," never did result in such a showing, excerpts from the White court's opinion, precedent to this day, copiously exhibit a desperate attempt to rationalize a despotic government's claim to power over life itself.

> Compelled military service is neither repugnant to a free government nor in conflict with the constitutional guaranties of individual liberty. Indeed, it may not be doubted that the very conception of a just government and its duty to the citizen includes the duty of the citizen to render military service in case of need and the right of the government to compel it.

> The power of Congress to compel military service as in the Selective Draft law, clearly sustained by the original Constitution, is even more manifest under the Fourteenth Amendment, which, as frequently has been pointed out, broadened the national scope of the government by causing citizenship of the United States to be paramount and dominant instead of being subordinate and derivative, thus operating generally upon the powers conferred by the Constitution.

> The highest duty of the citizen is to bear arms at the call of the nation. This duty is inherent in citizenship; without it and the correlative power of

the State to compel its performance society
could not be maintained.

It is a contradiction in terms to say that the
United States is a sovereign and yet lacks this
power of self-defense. Hence, the power was expressly granted by the Constitution. It is found in
the power to declare war, which means a power
to carry on war successfully, i.e., with the means
necessary.

There is no provision limiting the means to voluntary enlistment. On the contrary, Congress is
expressly empowered to use all means necessary
and proper to carry out the express grant. Hence,
the power to resort either to voluntary enlistment or to enforced draft is express.

Selective draft is not only an appropriate means
but under the conditions of modern warfare the
most prudent, just, and equitable method which
can be employed. That the power to compel military service is an incident of sovereignty ap-
pears from the custom of nations. Compulsory
service is now exacted by practically all the nations of the globe.

Several of the States, in ratifying the
Constitution, proposed amendments to limit the
power of Congress to raise armies by draft, and
their rejection shows not only that the language
employed was intended to include the power to
draft but also that this was the contemporary
interpretation.

In *Kneedler v. Lane, supra*, the Conscription Act of

1863, was sustained under the power to raise
armies; and in *United States v. Scott* and *United
States v. Murphy*, that act was construed, no question of its constitutionality being raised. Under
the similar clause in the Constitution of the Con-
federacy, draft acts were sustained in the confederate courts. Compulsory militia service has also
been enforced by the courts.

The status of a citizen properly drafted and that
of one who has voluntarily enlisted are the same.
Our armies have served in all parts of the world,
and such service has never been regarded illegal.

Compulsory military service is not contrary to
the spirit of democratic institutions, for the
Constitution implies equitable distribution of
the burdens no less than the privileges of citizenship. Whatever the limitations sought to be set
upon the Crown, there can be no doubt that
power to impress for foreign service resided in
Parliament, and was actually exerted.

The law imposes neither slavery nor involuntary
servitude. The Thirteenth Amendment was intended to abolish only the well-known forms of
slavery and involuntary servitude akin thereto,
and not to destroy the power of the Government
to compel a citizen to render public service.

Although I am confident there are plenty of lawyers
who could spend days salivating over these beside-the-
point rationalizations in the same way there are philoso-
phers still uncertain whether the cat is *on* the mat, separate
from the mat, integral *to* the mat, or actually even a cat on

an actual mat, nary a one is worthy of contemplation beyond "Should we file this under 'Nonsense'? 'Drivel'? Or
'Tragedy'?"

Challenges heard by the White court included (with
"it" referencing the Selective Draft): "that by some of its
administrative features it delegates federal power to state
officials;" "that it vests both legislative and judicial power
in administrative officers;" "that, by exempting ministers
of religion and theological students under certain conditions and by relieving from strictly military service members of certain religious sects whose tenets deny the moral
right to engage in war, it is repugnant to the First Amendment, as establishing or interfering with religion;" and
"that it creates involuntary servitude in violation of the
Thirteenth Amendment."

Except for this last, such scattergun arguments are
not even peripheral to the only one that matters: the argument, *the principle*, that gave birth to the Republic of
America.

The Covid Ruse

Question: What do "the draft" and "Covid" have in
common?

Answer: Government's claim to absolute control over
the life of the individual.

Although I recognized before "Covid" the potential
for an alleged health crisis to be used by petty tyrants who
believe that controlling their betters gives import to their
own empty existence, it wasn't until I witnessed the enforced idiocy of medically useless mask mandates, "social
distancing" (what chump concocted *that* term?), falsified

death certificates, claims of asymptomatic transmission, and societal-economic incarceration, that I began to suspect a scam. But when I read a three-paragraph article buried in the back pages of an American newspaper about how, "inexplicably," not a single case of flu had been reported in the state where that newspaper was published, I became certain Covid was, at the very least, a scam.

When I researched flu statistics in other states and countries, I encountered the same phenomenon.

The flu had vanished.

Brian C. Joondeph, MD, wrote in *American Thinker* in May 2021:[3]

> Seasonal influenza, also known as "the flu," visits America every year, similar to tornadoes, thunderstorms, heat waves, and snowstorms. As tracked by the CDC, over the past decade symptomatic flu cases ranged from 9 to 45 million cases per year in the U.S. Hospitalizations varied from 140 to 810 thousand, and deaths from 12 to 61 thousand, depending on the particular year, strain of influenza, and effectiveness of the vaccine.
>
> This year, "flu activity is unusually low" according to CDC surveillance. Since September 2020, the CDC recorded only about 2000 cases, a fraction of the tens of millions of cases in past years.
>
> Hospitalizations this flu season are minimal, with only 224 confirmed influenza hospitalizations from September 2020 to mid-April 2021 — nowhere near the hundreds of thousands of hospitalizations in past seasons. Deaths are harder to measure since the CDC changed how

deaths are characterized this past year. Instead of pneumonia, influenza, and Covid being in separate categories, now it's called PIC, lumping the three entities together.

The observant doctor listed asinine official speculation and posited a few facetious theories, then asked, "The CDC wouldn't play numbers games, would they?" And then answered, "Sure they would. The CDC changed its [PCR-test] cycle threshold for 'vaccine breakthrough cases' — cases occurring post-vaccination — to 28, far below that for pre-vaccination cases specifically to reduce the number of Covid cases reported after vaccination."

Dr. Joondeph concluded with a question that should by now be obvious to anyone paying attention.

"Was it ever really about a virus?"

Of course not. But worldwide compliance to scripted response mandates — masks, distancing, quarantine, lockdown, lethal treatment protocols, and immune-system-demolishing "vaccines" — provided an unprecedented indicator of people's willingness to do what they are told when overwhelmed by fear, so the ploy *will* be repeated. The next "pandemic" — Smallpox, Ebola, Ukraine Fever, Covid 25, Omicron 2 — is on dozens of calendars, as was Covid 19 long before it "appeared." (Everyone knows that *Omicron* was a 1963 sci-fi flick about an alien life form inserting itself, virus-like, into an Earthling . . . don't they?[4])

Of all the questions the Covid ruse should have inspired at every stage and on every level of its infestation, one tops the list and unmasks every other.

Why did a flu-like virus with minuscule lethality cue Soviet-style censorship?

Sooner or later, every dark plan must come out of the shadows to claim its prize. Thanks to the overt playing of the Covid card and the courage of a growing number of independent-thinking men and women who do not tremble before pathetic little bullies, the light of awareness is illuminating once-dark corners. To stand in that light, to open one's eyes and mind to what can be seen and known, to refuse to comply with the will of sociopaths and fools in certain knowledge that the only power evil can possess is that which the good gives it, is the first step toward taking justice back from evil hands.

Conscripting the Conscriptors

The Constitution of the United States of America, sans its antithetical amendments, is the supreme law of our land. As such it stands as a legal axiom, and as such the practice of passing today's legal buck to judges who yesterday tried similar cases or to what has previously been accepted or not struck down elsewhere, stands as an evasion. Certainly a perusal of like-kind precedents can be instructive and constructive, but only as an aid to determination, not as a standard of, or justification for, determination.

Without their cloddish references to immaterial prior legal findings, international customs, state proposals, Confederate Constitution inclusion, court enforcement, unspecified-entity "regard," and Crown limitations, Supreme Court justices in 1918 had only the axiom of the supreme law of the land against which to measure the Selective Draft Law — which was and is as it should be. Their laughably ham-handed attempt to alienate the supreme inalienable right provided a glaring, if unintended, additional precedent: proof of the corruptibility of the highest court in the land.

Every jurist on that bench, every concurring jurist since, and every politician and bureaucrat in their camp deserves to have his or her name printed on a slip of paper to be placed in a jar and withdrawn at random by the hand of a would-be military conscript. Following this "most prudent, just, and equitable method" of selection, these conscriptors would then be trained, armed, and transported to a designated arena for a *Hunger Games*-style to-the-death purification.

Utilizing Chief Justice Edward White's interpretive model, such a culling can surely be found constitutional.

It is as well that justice is blind.
Could she see, she would despair of
what has been done in her name.

Anonymous

2

THE UNFOUNDING

America was an idea brought to fruition by men who understood that human beings, in order to live *as human beings*, must be free and self-responsible. Their theory of inalienable rights, the idea that life and rights are inextricably entwined, provided the basis for a system wherein no man or government could be permitted to violate, oppress, or deny those rights. Never before had a nation been created in recognition of the needs, material and spiritual, of human life. Never before had a nation been created in acknowledgment of the value of the sovereign human person, and the original rules set forth for protecting this value were, and remain to this day, as close to ideal as have ever been composed.

But it took only three generations for America to drift toward an authoritarianism she was created to forever prohibit, and with increasing velocity another six to become an incongruous mongrel her founders would not today recognize as even an American species. No one person or political party threw a switch that changed a self-sustaining, life-furthering idea into a buffet for parasites and cannibals. One "minor" compromise at a time over time was all it took. One "insignificant" rights violation or emergency remedy or for-your-own-good resolution or "temporary" unconstitutional expedient or self-contradictory Constitution amendment propped open the door to permanent "tolerable" rights violations and liberty-razing norms.

As an idea, America is today an all-but-forgotten echo. As a nation, she is a shadow of what she was meant to be.

Can such an idea, representing such a nation, be restored incrementally beginning yet again from a premise that unconditionally esteems individual liberty? Can what was lost be reclaimed by reversing the progression of loss? Are contemporary Americans capable of uncompromisingly honoring the principles that made America possible? Are they capable of resolutely reinstating and abiding by the original constitutional blueprint that, despite decades of accumulated government-foisted trumpery and counterfeit ornamentation, *defines* America?

The Second of July

Two hundred and forty-eight years ago, on the third day of July 1776, John Adams wrote in a letter to his wife:[1]

> . . . the Delay of this Declaration to this Time has many great Advantages attending it. The Hopes of Reconciliation, which were fondly entertained by Multitudes of honest and well meaning though weak and mistaken People, have been gradually and at last totally extinguished. Time has been given for the whole People maturely to

consider the great Question of Independence
and to ripen their judgments, dissipate their
Fears, and allure their Hopes . . . so that the
whole People in every Colony of the 13 have now
adopted it, as their own Act.

About this Act, this unprecedented Declaration of
Independence, Adams declared: "The Second Day of July
1776, will be the most memorable Epocha, in the History
of America."

A final version of the document was adopted on July
fourth and signed by the delegates on August second.
When or if it was ever presented to King George remains
both unclear and unimportant for one reason: America's
Declaration of Independence was not penned primarily to
serve as notice to an oppressive government, but as a rallying cry for those whose rights had been oppressed by
government and as a statement of unified moral rectitude.

The principles responsible for breaking the chains of
human oppression are required in equal measure to prevent the reestablishment of oppression. Tragically, Adams'
"multitudes of honest and well meaning though weak and
mistaken people" have been patiently returned to the status of the hopefully conciliatory. Since the manufacturers
of chains for human oppression rely not on principles but
on the absence of principles, on a citizenry's acquiescence
to the wearing of oppression's chains, the most memorable epoch in the history of America has been archived
under The Merely Historical.

The nation of America has been *un*founded. The
proof, however inopportune, is irrefutable.

While We were Sleeping

To understand America's rarely checked journey toward
the abyss of statism, a bygone assumption should first be
revealed and contextually updated. No one has stated the
far-reaching implications of this assumption more plainly
than did Isabel Paterson in 1943 when she wrote:[2]

> The axiom of the Declaration of Independence
> that all men are endowed by their Creator with
> the inalienable right to life is now probably read
> by many Americans as a truism which never
> could have been denied. On the contrary, in that
> statement it was laid down for the first time as
> the political principle of a nation. It is the pri-
> mary postulate of the Society of Contract.
>
>   In the Society of Contract man is born free,
> and comes into his inheritance with maturity. By
> this concept all rights belong to the individual.
> Society consists of individuals in voluntary asso-
> ciation. The rights of any person are limited only
> by the equal rights of another person.
>
>   In the Society of Status nobody has any
> rights. The individual is not recognized; a man is
> defined by his relation to the group, and is pre-
> sumed to exist only by permission. The system
> of status is privilege and subjection. By the ulti-
> mate logic of the Society of Status, a member of
> the group who has not committed even a minor
> offense might be put to death for "the good of
> society."
>
>   In the Society of Status everyone is under
> obedience from the cradle to the grave; except,

by the same logic, a ruler whose will may be supreme, and who is therefore exempt from all obligations. He can do no wrong.

The logic of status ignores physical fact. The vital functions of a living creature do not wait upon permission and unless a person is already able to act of his own motion, he cannot obey a command. The Society of Status claims the power of life and death but in fact only persons have the gift of life. The claim of the Society of Status is actually based on the group power to inflict death.

As I explained in "The Pitiful Push," government's ultimate argument is a gun. The fact that this gun was constitutionally assigned to protect not "the government" but private citizens from criminals *and* government is a memory so distant it resembles myth. Choices and actions that in an unstructured moral society need pass only the personal scrutiny of, "Am I right to do this?" can in a Society of Contract reasonably become, "Am I legitimately prohibited from doing this?" But in a Society of Status the question is always, "Do I have *permission* to do this?" — with permission required for more and more of life's necessities. By the time "liberty" has been popularly reduced in conversation to "liberties," it is well on its way to being transformed from an inalienable right into a privilege permitted, parceled, and dispensed by government.

To ensure that a Society of Contract does not deteriorate into one of Status, and to prevent liberty from redefinition as Crown-apportioned endowments, constitution-delimited law is necessary.

Isabel Paterson clarifies:[3]

If everyone were invariably honest, able, wise,
and kind, there should be no occasion for government. Everyone would readily understand
what is desirable and what is possible in given
circumstances, all would concur upon the best
means toward their purpose and for equitable
participation in the ensuing benefits, and would
act without compulsion or default . . . But since
human beings will sometimes lie, shirk, break
promises, fail to improve their faculties, act im-
prudently, seize by violence the goods of others,
and even kill one another in anger or greed, government might be defined as the police organization. In that case, it must be described as a
necessary evil. It would have no existence as a
separate entity, and no intrinsic authority; it
could not be justly empowered to act excepting
as individuals infringed one another's rights,
when it should enforce prescribed penalties.
Generally, it would stand in the relation of a witness to contract, holding a forfeit for the parties.
As such, the least practicable measure of government must be the best. Anything beyond the
minimum must be oppression.

America's original Constitution was as near-perfect a
document as had ever been penned to preserve a Society
of Contract. Post-1791 congressional doctoring, however,
apart from Amendment XIII's prohibition of involuntary
servitude, "constitutionalized" America's unfounding.

Amendment XI resuscitated the Declaration-quashed
British common law dictum that "the King can do no
wrong." That this treachery immediately follows the Bill of
Rights is particularly offensive.

Because of The Founders' first-hand necessarily violent defense against a government's usurpation of rights, there is no constitutional warrant for Amendment XIV's inclusion of rebellion or insurrection. Did Congress in 1866 forget the unforgettable first and fourth sentences of their nation's 1776 formal rallying cry? Did it slip their little minds that their republic and Constitution were *born* of righteous rebellion? Or were the chains of authoritarianism being reforged even then and *by them*?

With Amendment XVI, passed in 1909 and ratified four years later while a private banking cartel was being installed and deceptively titled the "Federal Reserve,"[4] Congress granted itself the authority to tax citizen income, thereby annexing not only taxation's practical use as a tool of terror, control, and destruction, but the ethical implication that The State may claim power over the individual's power to provide for his own life.[5]

Amendment XVIII, the brazenly authoritarian prohibition of alcoholic-beverage manufacture ratified in 1919, was superficially repealed fourteen years later by the unrepentant Amendment XXI. This repeal was merely cosmetic because the legal and moral precedent advanced by XVIII had already been achieved and total control of a popular item of commerce, along with the retention of countless bureaucratic jobs, was, like a "be grateful we let you keep something" swindle, ensconced.

And the obscure "promote the general welfare" construction used in preamble gave every subsequent "for the public welfare" scheme legal teeth, however dull. In the spirit of constitutional intent it should have read, "prevent *the restriction* of the general welfare."

What Isabel Paterson observed eight decades ago — that inalienable rights were regarded by many Americans as an undeniable truism — metamorphosed as descendant

Americans slumbered through the transmutation of their inalienable rights into domestic-terrorist thought crime.

Incrementalism has time and again proven itself to be the Master of Takeover without so much as disturbing the dreams of its quarry, but while "Republican" politicians obediently perpetuate the Political Pendulum, even earth-quake-scale rights-toppling crises fail to rouse Americans from sleep to dress to America-saving action.

Billy Falcon's 2021 ballad, "Sleeping Giant," provides a poetic example of the tragedy of philosophically rootless frustration.[6] The spirit of his musical plea evokes passion and hope, the *feeling* of what America was meant to be, of what snoozing Americans have allowed to slip from waking grasp. Falcon's earnestness inspires tears of pride, but what should dry those tears and set jaws in anger is *knowing* that the power today's awakened Americans have on their side is only a feeling, and *knowing* that feelings are incapable of restoring the Republic of America.

When Mr. Falcon sings, "Smell the blood of freedom, if we don't stop the bleeding, they'll grind our bones to make their bread," he sings not of a conditional "if" but of an historical conclusion. The bleeding has for almost half of America's life been a hemorrhage, and Mr. Falcon's bones-to-bread metaphor has been more than a metaphor for just as long.

The sleeping giant exists. It is fat, dependent, and anemic. Worse, even if its waking was not shackled by normalcy bias, situation-ignorance, habituated lassitude, and a propensity for evidence denial and responsibility transference, it is armed with the wrong intellectual ammunition.

Give Us Liberty or Give Us . . . Stuff

In "Closing One Eye and Believing with the Other" I said I did not know when politician wannabees discovered that the way to get elected had nothing to do with moral integrity or competency and everything to do with telling "the people" what they want to hear. I observed that the people seldom seem to comprehend that their response to hearing what they want should not be *yes* at the polls, but a skeptic's demand for answers to critical questions.

Obviously, foremost among what voters have wanted to hear was what *they* were going to get from the government, and the giving and getting became over time inventive and elaborate. From welfare relief to the passing of favorable legislation; from discounted loans and debt forgiveness to "free" education and health care; from lucrative contract guarantees to protectionist laws; from price caps to wage increases to employment tenure to bribeable agency oversight to bailout acts to Universal Basic Income — the granted-wish list not only grew exponentially, it became expected and normal.

"My administration created a gazillion jobs in only one term!" lies every lying politician seeking a second or seventh rehire while fools buy the lie with their votes and trade liberty for government-gifted stuff.

Governments create nothing.

Not jobs, opportunity, business, education, energy, transportation, science, health, or wealth. Government power lies solely in compulsion, in the coercive taking and redistributing of what individual human beings make possible. Isabel Paterson gave a rudimentary example fully applicable today:[7]

To ascertain what was the action of government,
its peculiar function, in such a sequence of actions as that of the Lewis and Clark expedition,
let all the factors and conditions be noted. The
wilderness was there, in the order of nature.
Many private persons had explored a great deal
of it. The knowledge and skill of the two named
explorers had been developed by themselves.
Why did they go to the government before making their expedition? To obtain funds and an official commission. What did the government do
that Lewis and Clark could not do? Expropriate
funds from other private persons, by taxes. The
supplies for the expedition came from private
production. The *action of government* was merely
expropriative.

And speaking of parasitism as a way of transferring
wealth from individuals who produce to an entitlement
class capable only of consuming by way of a governing
class capable only of taking, those who have swallowed the
death-and-taxes-certainty hook would do well to separate
and scrutinize the second part of that self-fulfilling witti-
cism. From the moment Congress legalized government
theft of productive ability by means of an income tax, a
quest for "what else can we tax?" was zealously undertaken
at every level of government. A scant four generations
later, taxation that would once have inspired armed revolt
is scarcely noticed, or when noticed is shrugged off with
an attitude the governing class encourages: "I don't like it
but what can I do? Guess I should vote for the other guy
next time."

Which, also encouraged by the governing class, keeps
the Political Pendulum hovering over irreversible statism

with every pass *in either direction.*

That once-tongue-in-cheek death-and-taxes maxim[8] has become in reality, pay or die. When any portion of what we produce is confiscated by government and given to persons to whom we would not voluntarily give, that portion of our *lives* is not our own. When our failure to pay a particular tax deprives us from owning, using, and enjoying *all* of what is our right to own, use, and enjoy — which means *everything* our rightfully earned pennies can acquire through trade with other producers — *life* has been made conditional upon taxation.

Thanks to the original-Constitution-defying income-tax amendment, the confiscation of what our efforts bring into existence means that in a five-day work week all of Monday and often Tuesday, and for some earners part of Wednesday are, by political decree, *not ours.* Those never-to-be-lived-again days, that week out of every month, those two-and-a-half to four months out of every year, *those nine to fifteen years out of our lives,* have not only been stolen and squandered but fundamentally used against us.

And this is merely what has been confiscated from the production side. When it comes time to trade what we have earned in increasingly worthless currency for what we can use to sustain or enhance our lives, state and municipal sales taxes further diminish the real-world value of our effort. To sate the insatiable ever-expanding governing class' gluttony for finding new ways to tax and new stuff on which to waste what it steals, its functionaries strain their limited creative capacity to conjure categories ripe for taxes, surtaxes, fees, charges, and surcharges.

Including . . .

Tobacco products, alcoholic beverages, hotel stays, sports-event attendance, Internet and telephone bills, air transportation, cable- and satellite-TV subscriptions, new-

and luxury-car purchases, automobile rentals, indoor tanning, ATM transactions, yacht and jewelry sales, "fatty" foods, soft drinks, and gifts.

Every such tax, surtax, fee, charge, and surcharge is a furtive pay-for-permission dodge implemented by allegedly private businesses strong-armed by government to perform collection services. We cannot smoke, drink, stay in a hotel, attend a baseball game, watch television, fly, search the web, make a phone call, buy certain categories of motor vehicle, rent certain categories of equipment, engage in certain categories of financial transactions with *our* money, or purchase various categories of services or products unless we first pay the tax, surtax, fee, charge, or surcharge assigned by government to that category.

Out-in-the-open pay-for-permission dodges include mandated government-issued licenses for marriage, business creation, driving, bicycling, boating, hunting, fishing, pet ownership, barbering, fingernail manicuring, plumbing, roofing, carpentry, electrical wiring, dog training, property appraisal, food preparation, landscaping, gardening, alternative-energy-system installation, and even rainwater collection.

There are building-permit fees, building-inspection fees, well-permit fees, zoning-permit fees, car-license and ownership-transfer fees, gun-ownership and carry-permit fees, tourism and concession fees, business-registration fees, business-registration-renewal fees, public-land-use-permit fees, park-admission fees, off-road-vehicle-/boat-/airplane-registration fees, online-payment-of-fees fees — refusal of which to fork over means no building, no drinking from a well, no travel, no Second Amendment, no commerce, and no utilization of land owned by everyone and no one.

The ludicrous carbon-footprint tax is, by the standard

of the foregoing, no more outlandish than any other as-yet-unimplemented possibility, from taxing radishes and roses, body weight and calories consumed, cubic feet of air breathed per annum, pizza delivery, woodstove use, free-speech word count, and headstone engraving.

And then there is the so-called death tax, worthy of only one observation: that its advocates comprise a particularly despicable strata within the governing class, sharing cocktails and hors d'oeuvres with those who would mandate medical procedures and military-servitude conscription, every one of whom deserves punishment prohibited by America's Constitution.

Question: What does exorbitant cellular-level taxation have to do with the title of this chapter?

Answer: From whence do recipients of government-gifted stuff think the stuff comes?

Everything dispensed by government must first be taken from one person before it can be given to another. Since governments create nothing they can distribute only what they seize. The moment the income-tax amendment was put into play the Republic of America transformed from a land of opportunity made possible by autonomous entrepreneurial effort to a fiefdom of purloined handouts.

America is today the world's best-dressed bankrupt fence of stolen goods.

Unlike Patrick Henry's heroic proclamation, "Liberty or Stuff" is the whimper of flunkies and bootlickers. Not surprisingly, it was and continues to be a whimper heard, welcomed, and promiscuously granted by elected men and women who would unhesitatingly raid their neighbor's apple tree so that they can pretend to be providers of free apples.

Proof of Life?

The health of a person can be measured in three realms against two standards. The realms are physical, mental, and emotional-spiritual. The standards are comparative: one in statistical relation to an approximate human average; the other in relation to the particular unique person's personal best.

But what of the health of a nation?

Does a border-defined assemblage of persons, families, towns, cities, counties, and states similarly possess a body, mind, spirit? While only a Socialist would attempt to argue for the existence of a collective stomach or brain, a nation *is* a living organism and demonstrably representative of the general life-condition of its population. And nations are as distinguishable from one another as are the individual persons who comprise them.

Again, Isabel Paterson:[9]

> Territorial sovereignty is delimited by the
> boundaries. This is the virtue of nationalism; it is
> a spatial restriction on political power, an ulti-
> mate safeguard for the individual, a chance of
> escape from local tyranny. The rise of "interna-
> tionalism" always connotes a corresponding en-
> croachment on personal liberty; but it really
> does so by leaving no sovereignty anywhere.

America's wide-open-by-design southern border is a crisis for this reason. The authoritarian-collectivist Left are rabidly opposed to American borders because Leftists are rabidly anti-individual, anti-liberty, and anti-life. Persons, families, towns, cities, counties, states, and nations are each, within whatever greater whole they are sub-sumed, living organisms, and their health is measurable so long as health is objectively defined.

While America, like any other nation, can be statisti-cally compared to approximate other-nation averages, the true measure of her health can be determined only in re-lation to her personal best as defined by the source of her life and guarantor of her health. Since America is not her physical or incidental trappings, but the formalized ideas that brought her uniquely into existence as a nation, she has for decades been a disease-riddled organism depen-dent on and animated by a haphazard fragile array of life-support tools. That she is walking still, however aimlessly, is due exclusively to the power of the source of her life — her Declaration and Constitution — and to the remnants of a feeling for what made that source possible.

This is as conclusive a fact as has ever existed. The contagion that brought America to this condition infected and still infects her every vital organ.

Is it possible to restore life to a body in so advanced a state of decrepitude? Let us examine the fitness of the parts that comprise the whole, the recovery capacity of an organism *given at birth* the means to remain healthy, and, most importantly, the structure of the spirit that inspires the will to live.

Ayn Rand wrote both respectfully and regretfully of what she called "the specifically American sense of life."[10]

"A sense of life," she explained, "is a preconceptual equivalent of metaphysics, an emotional, subconsciously integrated appraisal of man and of existence. It represents an individual's unidentified philosophy" and "affects his choice of values and his emotional responses, influencing his actions and frequently clashing with his conscious con-victions."

Herein lies the reason that modern American patriotism, so poignantly and movingly demonstrated in these years of accelerating descent into the hell America was founded to prevent, will fail to do more in the big picture than steal another hour or two of liberty.

"A nation, like an individual," Miss Rand wrote in 1971, "has a sense of life."[11]

> [It] is formed by every individual child's early impressions of the world around him: of the ideas he is taught and of the way of acting he observes and evaluates. And although there are exceptions at both ends of the psychological spectrum — men whose sense of life is better or worse than that of their fellow citizens — the majority develop the essentials of the same subconscious philosophy. This is the source of what we observe as "national characteristics."

Which is the second reason America's Public Enemy Number One is public education. Miss Rand continued in the same essay:

> In order to form a hypothesis about the future of an individual, one must consider three elements: his present course of action, his conscious convictions, and his sense of life. The same elements must be considered to form a hypothesis about the future of a nation.

Were we to generally diagnose our republic's health by taking her societal temperature, we would find it hot, perhaps feverish. Heart and respiratory rate? Fluctuating according to "the news." Blood pressure? Elevated. Vision and hearing? Acute within a predetermined range of "the acceptable." Body-mass index? Corpulent. Reflexes? Sluggish. Medications? And then some. Vaccinations? Whatever the doctor orders.

Were we to seek diagnostic specificity by examining symptoms potentially indicative of a fundamental health problem, we would reference the barometer of culture — the ideas, achievements, influences, politics, education, behaviors, art, and entertainment that dominate American life — and we would find . . . what?

American men obsessed with watching, cheering for, betting on, and outfitting themselves in the costumes of professional game players is a sad manifestation of substitute masculine efficacy. That sports icons can command in a year more money than many of their fans will make in a lifetime speaks not primarily to athletic prowess or competitive skill, but to the confused value hierarchy of their audience. Of course there is nothing wrong with making bags of money for playing a game at which one has aptitude and talent, but when fans vicariously experience personal efficacy through *symbols* of efficacy, a deeper cultural problem exists.

Sports-hero fixations, however, are at least reality-based circus-games distractions.

Americans spend just under seven hours a day in a virtual world — forty-four percent of their waking time — and not in the performance of online business. Two-and-a-half hours are dedicated to media deceitfully called "social" and designed to be both addictive and privacy-eliminating while reducing human interaction to the two-dimensional, with up to four point two hours playing mobile games. Add three-and-a-third hours of television to the mix and across a seventy-five-year lifetime, forty-eight waking *years* will have been spent staring at glowing rectangles.

What, I had to ask and learn, is so irresistibly attractive in the virtual universe?

First, a caveat.

I stopped watching television in 1996. I am reminded why whenever I curiously flip through hotel-TV channels. Accordingly, I lack the temperament necessary for calmly expounding the nihilistic nonsense Americans apparently consider entertaining. Furthermore, my use of the Internet is limited to business, research, news gathering, supplies purchases, and some correspondence, averaging between six and ten gigabytes of data used per month. That said, for the purpose of sampling what I am missing I dedicated several days to exploring a pixelated smorgasbord.

I read a dozen or so up-to-the-minute reports about social-media personalities, variously describing popularity, wealth, personal attributes, and accolades. I learned that numerous virtual-world icons began their climb to millions-of-followers stardom by lip-syncing other people's music. I learned that there are hundreds of millions of real-world human beings anxiously awaiting what Kylie Jenner, Rihanna, Kanye West, Busy Philipps, Baby Ariel, Kim Kardashian, Brent Rivera, Bella Poarch, and Swag-BoyQ have to say about beauty, music, fashion, gadgets, lifestyle, and what they had for lunch and with whom. I learned that there are Internet celebrities famous for commenting on games and staging "pranks" and issuing "challenges."

I learned about a pair of twenty-something brothers who six years ago had thirty-three million subscribers on YouTube, twenty-seven million followers on Instagram, twenty-one million fans on Facebook, and a combined net worth of $23 million. Except for their announcement of future T-shirt and hoodie sales, I was unable to discover what the duo actually did for a living. The brothers' dead-from-the-neck-up promotional photo revealed that one had malformed fingers, as if recently shut in a car door, but further research disclosed the disfigurement as wide-spread among celebrities who "rap."

Prompted several months earlier by a friend who asked, "Why would America's most popular patriotic voice give two hours of interview time to an ignoramus?" I had already researched a former competitive kick-boxer who sells to admiring males advice on how to get the bod, the babe, the buggy, and the bounty they desire. Although I had previously heard the term "toxic masculinity," it was not until personally observing the follower-garnering wis-dom of Andrew Tate that I could reconcile such an awk-ward word pairing. Certainly this blowhard offered multi-ple reasons for the label's creation, but while his toxicity was copious, "masculinity" had been misapplied.

I learned that the fluff of social media is called "con-tent" and that those who make the fluff are called "content creators" which, given the junk-food emptiness of this fodder for the mentally flaccid, seemed an apt descriptor. And, unfortunately, I learned about social-media "influ-encers," a term I can only regard as a vocabulary adapta-tion for the mentally flaccid and that I will not be adding to my word processor's dictionary.

(I also realized that content creation and influencer describe what will be AI's contribution to Information Age 2.0, that the planners are just planning ahead.)

Throughout this dutiful immersion I kept in mind Sheriff Bell's concern in Cormac McCarthy's *No Country for Old Men*.[12] The Sheriff speculated that by pushing his chips forward and going out to meet something he doesn't understand, a man "would have to put his soul at hazard."

Eighteen hours was as much as I could bear.

Computer applications automatize tasks that once required focused thought, eliminating conscious cause-and-effect connection. So-called artificial intelligence, which can never replicate the distinctively human act of creation, is rapidly being infused into every level of research, communication, study, and business while meeting little resistance. Over time, even those who sense there is something wrong with machine "thinking," fully intended to replace human thinking, are likely to hit the "Let AI compose your [fill in the blank]" button.

Our personal motorized transport more and more takes over from the moment we press *start* to the moment a computerized voice welcomes us to our destination. Seven out of ten Americans depend on government-service monopolies for life's taken-for-granted necessaries: electric power, water delivery, sewage disposal, and garbage-removal. We allow the crooked FDA to control what we eat and the crooked USDA, aided by brain-dead order-following federal, state, and local law-enforcement goons, to prevent us from making our own decisions about where we obtain what we eat. We casually pop pills to relieve the symptoms of ailments, both legitimate and industry concocted, and to ease the strain of reality.

In short, in addition to gluttonously relishing the cognitive ingestion of fluff, Americans have become convenience junkies habituated to grabbing whatever will allegedly make life "easier" while bypassing the question, "What am I trading for yet another layer of ease?" and the obvious, "That something *can* be done does not mean it *should* be done."

Only an independent-minded citizenry, which means an independence-capable citizenry, can preserve a free independent nation. But the dominant feature of American culture today is *de*pendence, and the *enough* I referenced in "Easy Street" applies not only to ease but to memory, tolerance, and the *de facto* endorsement of wrongdoing.

The admirably unforgiving scene at the close of the aforementioned *Judgment at Nuremberg* humanizes this point. Convicted Nazi jurist Ernst Yanning asks the trial's presiding judge to come to his prison cell. Judge Haywood obliges and Yanning appeals to his American counterpart, "Those people, those millions of people, I never knew it would come to that." To which Judge Haywood calmly replies, "Herr Yanning, it came to that the first time you sentenced a man to death you knew to be innocent."[13]

Americans and their political representatives are cognizant of dozens, if not hundreds, of unforgivable State-orchestrated violations of Constitution-protected rights, including murder and acts of America-destruction. It is not their number that is unforgivable, but the fact that even one of these violations has been excused and/or concealed by government lies and then buried beneath timely political distractions and, except by stalwart seekers of justice and those whose lives have been shattered, forgotten.

In recent history alone, Operation Northwoods,[14] the John F. Kennedy assassination,[15] Gulf of Tonkin incident,[16] Ruby Ridge[17] and Waco[18] assaults, Oklahoma City bombing,[19] 9/11,[20] Las Vegas-concert shooting,[21] Covid ruse, and J6 protest[22] with its example-execution of Ashley Babbitt remain as current and, where justice is concerned, as unsettled as at the time of their staging.

The moment government was exposed as potentially complicit, these criminal deceptions warranted the immediate cessation of all other government business. Every politician who failed to meaningfully proclaim, "We will conduct no 'business as usual' until this travesty has been made right and those responsible for its perpetration have been brought to justice," is responsible for betraying the reason our constitutional republic was instituted. There can morally be no new business — no welfare-program debates, no foreign-diplomat meetings, no overseas-war-funding discussions, no infrastructure-rebuilding vote — *no new business* — until State-sanctioned wrongs have been made right and the perpetrators *brought to unforgiving justice* no matter how wide the gap between commitment and discovery.

Are America's government functionaries too busy to constitutionally represent Americans? Are there too many pies in their government-approved gas ovens? Did it have to come to this?

Yes. Yes. And, yes.

America's government functionaries *are* too busy — violating the rights of their citizen employers. They *do* have too many pies in the oven — with their fingers in most of them. *And it came to this the first time they failed to aggressively make right a single government-sanctioned wrong.*

"Investigations" into State crimes, from the FBI's "thorough and professional investigation into the responsibility of Lee Harvey Oswald for the [JFK] assassination" to the mendacious 9/11 Commission Report to the J6 Select Committee clown show, are cover-story official "answers" to "do something" demands.

What was the long-term consequence of the seemingly bona fide 1975 Senator Frank Church probe into criminal CIA/NSA/FBI activity? The CIA's budget at the time was $750 million. Applying Edward Snowden's 2012-revealed twenty-eight percent CIA take of the National Intelligence budget, by 2023 it had risen to $20.2 billion. When adjusted for Federal Reserve-created inflation that amounts to a 560-percent performance *bonus* awarded to a Constitution-scorning America-dishonoring Treason Cell that should have been liquidated by 1976.

Which leads us to twin America-destroying attributes of our politician employees:

1) The wealth we allow them to compile, and

2) Our reliance on them to defend on our behalf what makes America, *America*.

"Generally speaking," wrote Isabel Paterson,[23]

> up to the Civil War any man seeking political honors expected to do so at some financial loss to himself; he lived by his private means. It is only when this condition prevails that men of intelligence, integrity, and good taste — the productive character — will be inclined to enter public life.

The riches amassed by today's upper-level politicians do not result from their ability to *create* wealth, but to *take* wealth through legislation, favor-swapping, lobbyist deals, corporate connections, insider information, and system manipulation. Their pledged constitutionally delimited citizen-representation responsibilities become secondary at best, and rights violations accumulate as an unrightable backlog. This is, of course, disastrous in itself, but what what makes it deadly to the sustaining of a constitutional republic is that it is accepted by an American citizenry with a shrug and a "What can we do?"

And yet, Americans continue to seek ballot-box solutions to ballot-box-created problems. They want *someone* to fix what is broken and they naïvely believe that voting for so-and-so is the answer. Prior to the Civil War, prior to unprofitable temporary political stints becoming lucrative life-long careers enjoyed by public servants unable to earn through independent effort, Americans did not expect to be rescued from life by a "leader." Americans were once, as individuals, their own leaders — which reconnects with sense of life and culture in the way Ayn Rand described:[24]

> A nation's culture is the equivalent of a man's conscious convictions. Just as an individual's sense of life can clash with his conscious convictions, hampering or defeating his actions, so a nation's sense of life can clash with its culture, hampering or defeating its political course. Just as an individual's sense of life can be better or worse than his conscious convictions, so can a nation's. And just as an individual who has never translated his sense of life into conscious convictions is in terrible danger — no matter how good his subconscious values — so is a nation.

"*This*," she concluded a half century ago, "is the position of America today."

A half century later, the aforementioned interviewer of the manly Mister Tate provided a clear sense-of-life-versus-conscious-convictions illustration. Tucker Carlson, upon sensibly telling his audience that they should "cling to [their] taboos" — meaning they should defend their personal moral standards against political subversion[25] — vitiated the soundness of his recommendation by explaining that "the taboos were organic; they derived from collective experience and instinct, the two most reliable guides to life." And, "You know the outlines of right and wrong; you were born knowing them."

What?

Humans know nothing at birth, never mind how to distinguish right from wrong, and "collective experience" does not a system of ethics make. Perhaps, I speculated at the time, the ordinarily insightful Carlson meant to say *reason* rather than *instinct*, but if the minds he reaches cannot accurately communicate and rationally defend the non-instinctual principles they desperately need to keep their values and lives, no matter how many skirmishes are won using inaccurate ammunition, the war will be lost.

Surely, I thought, the most popular patriotic voice in America knows this?

A few months later Carlson may as well have answered, "Nope, I don't," when publicly reiterating reliance on hooey. As reported by *Zero Hedge*:[26]

> Your gut is the one thing that doesn't lie to you. Your gut only has your interest in mind. It is not trying to sell you a product, or convince you to vote for it. I'm just telling you once again, what you already know, which is this is going to be — the next year is going to be, I think I'd bet my house on it, really like nothing we've ever seen in the country. And everyone can kind of feel that. You know, most of our perceptions come through intuition rather than reason. But if you're close to your dog, you know, the dog knows exactly what's going on . . . they just watch and they feel. And people are very much the same. And if something bad is about to happen, everybody gets jumpy. And everybody's really jumpy right now.

Neither Carlson's nor anyone's guts and intuition can defend against bad ideas and centuries-entrenched government corruption. Feelings will, on the other hand, motivate dependent minds to seek and settle for proxies anathema to the goals of America's founders.

In politics: surrogate leaders.

In philosophy: surrogate thinkers.

The wealth-accumulation potential in government is similarly available to upper-echelon occupiers of the talk-show trade, and although American show-host profits derive from market demand, bank accounts are boosted by the fall of America. Discussing political problems from behind a studio microphone may help to increase awareness, but even if talk-show celebrities were not so obviously bracketed by sponsor and ratings considerations, news-analysis numbness is as inevitable as Hollywood-violence numbness.

The current fashionable crop of vocal commandos — the whining Mark Levin, the former Obama-protector Dan Bongino, the gun-toting poster babe Dana Loesch — are the curative equivalent of throat lozenges: attractively packaged, palatably flavored, temporary-relief providing, and habit-forming. The bigger they get the louder they bark within authorized vision-handicapping constraints, with the biggest being the loudest and most vision handicapped.

How can anyone take seriously a man who boasts that he got Covid-vaccinated because President Trump told him to? Or who refers to his admirers as "Levinites"? Or who condescendingly implies that dissenters, some of whom possess knowledge The Great One is unable or unwilling to see, are wrong because they disagree or have sold fewer books? Or whose multimillion-copy-selling *American Marxism*, more than half of which consists of quotes from other authors, unifies *while conversationally normalizing* antithetical concepts tastelessly dust-jacketed between clip-art images of an American flag superimposed over a Communist Party hammer and sickle?

Today's overpopulated punditocracy ranges from establishment-authorized personalities to fly-by-night nut

jobs with a few truly original thinkers scattered throughout. Because of alternative media's disgraceful tendency to
assimilate the perceptual limits of mainstream media, independent journalists and researchers are the sole remaining fount of untainted information while they battle
censorship and extinction. Even so, America has become a
nation of watchers, and while watching can enlighten
within a certain cultural context, in another it can appease
and defuse.

Over the past two decades, novels and movies depict-
ing brave youngsters battling one or another version of totalitarian dystopia have become wildly popular. Despite,
however, the reasonable conclusion that target-audience
members recognize and esteem the virtues that inspire
their fictional counterparts to wage war against corruption
and oppression — freedom, justice, truth, honor, love —
these modern make-believe champions can exist *only* in
the pages of a book or on a screen manipulated by legions
of computer technicians.

In consequence, the values and causes for which they
fight become as unreal as their superhuman athletic prowess, lethal-injury-recuperation aptitude, self-replenishing
archery quivers, and limitless-capacity firearm magazines.

Fiction has the power to characterize virtues that can
be made real in the real world. Which is good. It also has
the power, when relegating virtuous ideals, goals, and action to fantasy-land, to fictionalize virtue itself.

Not good.

Over the past two centuries, like an inspired novel
that began with passionately motivated larger-than-life
characters but promptly fizzled into a soap opera laced
with cheap political and criminal intrigue, America became a model of everything she was created not to be.

She is grievously wrongly defined. Her just heart has

been cut out and reinstalled upside-down and backwards. The educational instrument of her ideological tomorrow is a black hole into which parents continue to sacrifice their children by the millions while, when expedient, handing them political banners. The means by which conversation, debate, ideas, news, and law are comprehensibly expressed has been robbed of meaning. Her government is gargantuan and debauched, and whatever vestige of goodness remains among its functionaries is negated by that particularly disgusting brand of spinelessness called "Just doing my job." Her militarized law-enforcement squads increasingly consist of amoral automatons who should be wearing the robot-mimicking Peacekeeper costumes of *The Hunger Games*.

Cells mistakenly assumed integral to the organism of America are not only unable to contribute to the life of America, but are a cancer draining life from America. The Central Intelligence Agency, Federal Bureau of Investigation, Department of Homeland Security, Drug Enforcement Agency, Food and Drug Administration, Bureau of Alcohol, Tobacco, Firearms and Explosives, Federal Trade Commission, Department of Education, *and all the rest* are corruptible-by-design tumors in the body of America to disable and destroy America. These implants cannot be "made better" in an effort to heal America because they are, themselves, disease.

Whether as a result of honest ignorance, willful stupidity, political influence, or blackmail, America's arbiters of justice have as a class betrayed the Constitution they swore to uphold. Sporadic Constitution-respecting rulings issue from courtrooms as crumbs tossed to a citizenry desperate for proof that America is still alive and grateful for a glimmer of hope. Jane Welsh Carlyle described the process in the mid-1800s: "When one has been threatened with a great injustice, one accepts a smaller as a favor." In the foreground, the Political Pendulum swings distractingly from Right to Left while in the background it relentlessly advances an acceptable "normal" from liberty to enslavement.

The crucifixion of the First Amendment is aided by fools clinging to their censoring social-media accounts. The January 6th 2021 non-insurrection will forever remain a regrettable mistake because it was *not* a confident retrieval of stolen goods, but an extemporaneous lukewarm display of discontent at having been robbed. The "What group do you belong to?" question, which would once have been met with a contemptuous sniff, will soon be asked on government-run-hospital admittance forms, bank-account paperwork, and North American Union ID applications. The concept "friend" has been demoted to a social-media verb. Our blue skies have been spray-painted white[27] with patented sun-dimming jet-dispersed particulates for decades and yet, when questioned by the handful of Americans who notice and care, the technology is repeatedly officially denied until, suddenly, former CIA director John Brennan and other professional liars begin publicly mentioning the technology as "promising." The Political Pendulum vacillates between twin anti-liberty possibilities, it's momentum assured by never-learning voters looking to be led or saved by political-theater posers. And while Americans complain and vote and believe what they want to hear while hoping to save their "democracy," talk-show big-shots blind to the destructiveness of making infotainment of America's death spasms ride the wave.

Then, lest we forget, there is the ultimate totalitarian deathblow: Make it impossible or illegal for Americans to defend their property, liberty, and lives against criminals on our streets and in government.

Lawmakers need not *ban* guns to be in violation of our Constitution's Second Amendment, they need only *infringe*, and there is no room for interpretation where the definition of infringement is concerned. Every loophole-exploiting, periphery-chiseling assault on factory, aftermarket, or gunsmith concepts that enhance the efficiency and accuracy of personal armament — from stock construction, magazine capacity, caliber and load specification, barrel length, sight configuration, and trigger design — is an infringement.

Add to Americans' willingness to endlessly participate in an argument exiled from its simple constitutional origin the unrelenting illegal assault on their right to personal self-defense, and the transformation from "America, Protector of the Right to Life, Liberty, and Happiness Pursued" to "America, Enemy of Americans" is complete.

Every now and again a fact of reality melds with a metaphor in a way that is poetically flawless and ethically just. America's forty-sixth "leader" is a physically decrepit, cognitively vacuous, morally corrupt, ludicrously incoherent, brazenly treasonous, rotting husk of a propped-up criminal parasite. As Oscar Wilde's portrait of Dorian Gray reveals what becomes of Dorian Gray, Joseph Robinette Biden *is* what has become of our constitutional republic.

Americans are no longer citizens, but subjects, more than half of whom don't mind being subjects while too many of those remaining believe that the answer to a presidential cadaver is a reality-show actor-opportunist who, compared to the men who made America possible is a spoiled boy.

The first step toward recovery from any condition of critical diminution is to unsparingly name the condition.

To that end:

America is not in decline. America is gone.

Pretending otherwise has become a national pastime.

Good Ol' Days

This "countdown to too late" concluded long ago at the same time political action no longer had the power to stop it. The so-called "Awakening" may be real, but it is an awakening of complacent passengers in a luxuriantly furnished dining car on a train that has for more than a century been speeding over rusty rails toward a dismantled bridge that once, through ingenuity born of unrestrained liberty, spanned the chasm of statist mediocrity.

The early-1900s proverb, "Shirtsleeves to shirtsleeves in three generations," referenced the fate of heirs unable to sustain a wealth-producing enterprise built from scratch by their forebears, but its application extends beyond business solvency. The heirs to what Isabel Paterson described as "the greatest inheritance man has ever enjoyed" frittered away what they could never have created. In addition to planting the two-party time bomb at the three-generations juncture, Americans allowed their government to shoot their constitutional republic in one foot with Amendment XI and in the other with Amendment XIV, then in both knees with the Sherman and Clayton Acts. They acquiesced to a bullet to the back when bending over for the federal income tax and, less than a year later, made it a double tap by okaying the Federal Reserve Act. After taking one to the gut by donating three million conscripts to the Great War before starving through a depression caused by federal fiscal policy, they all but wel-comed a bullet to the heart by failing to militantly refuse to hand over their gold to Franklin "New Deal" Roosevelt.

Bullet to the Head Number One was delivered when subjects bequeathed to their masters the authority to forcibly confiscate earnings in the name of "social secu-rity." Number Two when allowing Nixon to nix the gold standard. Three when fearfully obliging the Patriot Act and its rash of rights desecrations. Four with the patheti-cally appropriately nicknamed Obamacare. Five with sea-to-shining-sea acquiescence to societal lockdowns, mask mandates, business closures, and fake-virus non-vaccina-tions. Numbers Six through Thirteen with every million or so taxpayer-sponsored illegal border crossings. And making all of it possible is the get-them-while-they're-maleable system of indoctrination called public schooling.

Additional suicidal wounds merely insult a miserable demise, but Number Fourteen will be a tossup between central-bank-regulated digital currency, social-credit scor-ing, and carbon-footprint legislation. The finalé, however, will be a planet-enveloping satellite-surveillance control grid managed by whoever programs artificial intelligence, ultimately featuring human-AI integration.

Mature Americans have a mélange of reasons to rem-inisce fondly about the past. Simpler times, perhaps. The company of departed friends. Opportunities pursued. Pas-sions expressed. Love given. Love returned. The popular-ity of all things vintage speaks to a nostalgia for something good about about "the old days," and although the "some-thing" differs from person to person, one particular some-thing is shared by every mature American. Whether or not Yuri Bezmenov's "stretched in time" KGB subversion tech-nique is perceived, reminiscing Americans were freer a decade ago and freer still the decade before.

And because the good ol' days *were* freer days, reminiscence has become an act of gazing backwards from a darker and darker place of liberty lost.

Whistling Away the Dark

What remains of America today lives only in the minds and hearts of Americans who understand and respect the idea of Original America, and of those there are few.

Yes, there are observant thinkers capable of recognizing trouble, consequences, and conditions — of predicting, forecasting, and warning — of gathering, assembling, and presenting in context important hidden information — and probably there are some earnestly pro-America men and women in government, but here's the rub:

Revelations exposing new acts of government corruption are tantamount to piling additional bodies atop a count already incalculable, which is to say that beyond signing and publishing America's death certificate there is nothing to add that has not in principle already been said.

Except, of course, for the conversation our "representatives" in government long ago made illegal.

The alleged crime of "inciting violence" via speech is not a defense against violence, but an attack on speech. Ideologically it walks hand in hand with Amendment XIV's rebellion clause; legally it criminalizes America's Declaration of Independence. The presumption that adult men and women are incapable of judging what ideas are worthy of action and what ideas are not — and are too weak to accept responsibility for their judgment — underlies every "we know what's best" authoritarian decree.

The "incitement" of an act via speech — whether

kindness, charity, heroics, creation, marriage, theft, rape, murder, or rebellion — is a fallacy. Unless the incitees are children there is only good judgment, bad judgment, and action-ownership.

What is wrong this year was on track decades ago to be wrong this year, just as what was wrong decades ago was on track to be wrong decades before that. New books draw from old books the wisdom of what has already been said. The exquisitely clear writings of Paterson, Rand, Huxley, Locke, de Tocqueville, Jefferson, Paine, Orwell, and others provided more than enough intellectual ammunition to save America *but did not inspire Americans to save America*. And although wrongs inconceivable in their day have been revealed and contextualized by big-picture-cognizant researchers such as Whitney Webb, G. Edward Griffin, and David Icke, normalcy-bias-induced evidence rejection reduces crisis-preventing roadblocks of truth into mannerly speed bumps on a crisis-destined course.

Does it help or even matter that every statist plan has a built-in self-destruct feature? No, and not because statists understand that inspiration for creative production will evaporate the moment human beings are stripped of the conditions needed to live *as human beings*, but because statists desire destruction and death, including their own. Fear of a bad end does not enter into the statist psyche; only the whim is important.

"I want it to be true, therefore it must be."

Eighty-one years ago, Isabel Paterson described the premise for statist ascendancy:[28]

> When a dictatorship gains power, it is by various groups conceding the power piecemeal, not perceiving what it must add up to in the end. Men enslave themselves, forging the chains link by

link, usually by demanding protection as a
group. When businessmen ask for government
credit, they surrender control of their business.
When labor asks for enforced "collective bar-
gaining" it has yielded its own freedom. When
racial groups are recognized in law, they can be
discriminated against by law.

Eighty-one years later, former U.S. Senator Ron Paul
furnished an instructive example of politics divorced from
premises:[29]

President Biden's request for an additional $100
billion to spread around Ukraine, Israel, and Tai-
wan was rejected by a Congress eager for its win-
ter break, and with each passing day it looks like
it's going to be harder to push it through. Poll
after poll show that Americans are increasingly
opposed to more of their money being spent on
the neocon's lost-cause war to over-throw Putin
in Russia.

For example, a recent Fox News poll revealed
that more than 60% of Republican voters do not
want any more money sent to Ukraine. As we enter an election year, it's probably safe to predict
that Republican candidates will be wary of cross-
ing the wishes of the clear majority of voters.

Ukraine-war funding? Congressional recess? Fox News
polls? Republican-voter wishes? Election strategies? Presumably the former senator, a more intelligent and decent
person than most of his peers, recognizes an *it makes no
fucking difference* moment when he sees it?

Although it is not my intention to unfairly label a

journalistic observation as unphilosophical to advance a cause-versus-effect argument, this report is as relevant to the big picture as hairstyles are to heart attacks. Focusing on Ukraine, voter polls, and election-year strategies gives power to political theater while the real agenda advances. It is, as Henry Mancini musically portrayed in the 1970 Blake Edwards film, *Darling Lili*, whistling in the dark hoping to chase away the dark.

Miss Paterson's and Dr. Paul's observations contrastingly illustrate the relationship between an ideological premise and a political consequence, the difference between *curing* disease and popping symptom-relieving pills. And, yet, "neither quite knowing which way they are going," politicians and patriots alike continue to whistle.

Maybe if accompanied by a few hundred million gelded subjects of Amerizuela or AI-merica the dark will just go away?

"WAIT!" wafts an earnestly hopeful voice from the grandstand. "Is that it? Aren't you going to conclude with a note of optimistic encouragement? Like, 'now it's up to us' or 'yes we can' or 'build back bigger' or 'trust the plan' or 'faith in the American spirit will see us to brighter days'?"

No.

But don't worry. This very minute, all across America, Conservative talk-show personalities are caressing their listeners' normalcy bias and warning that America is in trouble and selling joint-pain relief, and almost to a fan their listeners feel assuaged and grateful and encouraged.

Besides, some overpaid circus-games gladiator just threw a touchdown pass in the Whatever Bowl.

WHAT CAN ONE TRUE AMERICAN DO?

If you are an American in the original sense of the word, if America's Declaration and Constitution mean to you what they meant to their courageous authors and you hold your life to be *yours*, you must draw a hard line around your free and sovereign person.

The second of July, 1776, was the day the Continental Congress voted to achieve independence from a tyranni-cal government, the day the idea of a free nation became a promise. It is worth stating again that America's Declara-tion of Independence was penned not primarily to give notice to an oppressive government, but as a reminder and rallying cry for those whose lives had been oppressed by government. It is equally important to note that it took only three generations for Americans' elected representa-tives to reintroduce the kind of authoritarian toxins our republic was created to reject. But crucial for identifying America's current position between the sunny shore of Constitution-protected liberty and the lightless depths of statism are honest answers to the following two questions. The first is historical and retrospective; the second, cur-rent and predictive.

What effort since 1776 has staid for more than a moment the steady abandonment of America's founding principles?

And . . .

What does a spotlight-addicted, favor-indebted, Executive Order-pimping, Israel-serving, nation-annexing, Father of the Toxic Vaccine chosen-by-God crony-capitalist billionaire and a hand-picked coterie of AI-enshrining, digital-money-obsessed, universal-basic-income-advocating, carbon-tax-touting, Israel-fawning, crony-capitalist billionaire advisors, accomplices, and czars have in common with the apostles of global totalitarianism?

The Minority of One

Most of us live in two worlds: the one that matters to us personally every day, and the one that surrounds us on the periphery. The first — the inner world of family and friends, work and education, art and entertainment, challenges and achievements, dreams and aspirations — leaves little time to critically scrutinize the outer world that governs or rules. Some Americans expect that the men and women they choose as representatives will be guardians of America's Constitution, as they have so sworn. Some expect them to do whatever voters want regardless of constitutional merit. Some don't trust anyone aspiring to political authority to do anything but serve and enrich themselves, cynically joking about the ever more commonplace immoral and illegal behavior of the ruling class.

Few Americans, however, can stay abreast of, never mind untangle and respond to, the tangled secret theater of this surrealistic outer world. There is simply too much information offered by too many sources and perspectives, too often with ulterior motives and tainted agendas. Pausing to contemplate such an outer world can be like standing in a frenzied crowd before an immense bulletin board crammed with overlapping notices, warnings, posters, pamphlets, business cards, photographs, and sticky notes — making it far easier to turn away unenlightened than to patiently sort through the chaos of *too much*.

And yet if we turn away overwhelmed and unenlightened from the threat this outer world poses or if we allow information "analysts" to do our reasoning for us, we risk losing everything that matters in our personal world. Those who conspire to collectivize individual human beings as a single neck for a government-held noose have, in their bag of psychological tricks, two certainties on which they rely.

First, they know that personal-life-focused men and women are likely to be overwhelmed and turn away unenlightened, leaving control of the outer world and future to *them*. Second, with neither understanding nor empathy they know that personal-life-focused men and women want to spend their days in pursuit of achievement, love, and happiness — immersed in the kind of values-rich life that liberty makes possible. Those who profit from controlling the lives of others, however, who have neither the strength nor the courage to live independently, regard living independently not as strength and an honorable full-time job but as an exploitable vulnerability waiting to provide *them* with full-time jobs.

Under the disingenuous banner of "serving the public," wannabe controllers seek roles as Chosen Ones benighted with the wisdom and power to decide "for the public" what is best for "the pubic," as if the public is not an association of independent, decision-capable sovereign persons responsible for living their own lives, but an unconscious helpless rabble in need of parental instructions and permissions. Over time, public-servant rule manifests as a dominant cultural condition.

Those who want only to productively and happily live can scarcely imagine, let alone take seriously, members of their own species whose ambition is to profit from controlling the lives of others, from confiscating what they cannot produce and distributing it to dependents of their choosing while, like parasites on commission, lining their pockets. Although moral men and women can imagine defending themselves against armed thieves, grasping the fact that their government representatives are system-protected armed thieves is foreign to their manner of coming at life, a naïveté that grants system-protected thieves immunity from the tar-and-feathering or rope-stretching appointments they deserve.

What can a minority of True Americans do in the face of a system-protected army of thieves grown so vast, so entrenched, so bolstered by an burgeoning complacent entitlement-mentality population of subjects?

Vote? Band together in groups and committees? Subscribe to independent news sources? Write opinion letters to newspaper editors? Comment anonymously on controversial subjects posted online? Complain among friends over beer or coffee? Run for political office? Take up arms? Pay homage on The Fourth to "what might have been" while resigned to rhetorically asking the universe, "What can one person do?"

Since America was brought into existence on the premise that human beings, to live *as human beings*, must be free and self-responsible, the principle implicit in what The Founders called inalienable rights is sacrosanct. Inalienable rights are absolute and nonnegotiable, no less so in the twenty-first century than in the eighteenth, and no man or government may be permitted to violate, oppress, deny, or "reinterpret" these rights. Inalienable, sacrosanct,

absolute, nonnegotiable rights are the foundation of America's Declaration of Independence and Constitution, of her identity and soul as a nation, of what it means to be "an American." Their methodical violation, oppression, denial, and reinterpretation by the very government created to preserve and defend them is an atrocity.

Americans who have not yet accepted the fact that their nation has been cannibalized beyond the point of death should give themselves a hearty pat on the back for their ability to either wrongly define America, ignore a superabundance of evidence accumulated across generations, or mulishly embrace normalcy bias. The heralded "Awakening" is too little too late and mired in the indoctrinated belief that politics is the answer. America will never be restored until Americans own five truths.

1) The Republic of America is gone. Not diminished or failing. Gone.
2) A restoration must be a resurrection, for it is from the grave that America must rise.
3) Such a resurrection would be an accomplishment as unprecedented in history as was America's birth, requiring no less dedicated or perilous a commitment.
4) The rubbish heap of American culture, the inconstancy of citizen fortitude, a horizon-to-horizon ignorance of what makes America, *America*, and hoards of convenience dependents, "just doing my job" functionaries, and stolen-money trough feeders combine with epidemic-scale normalcy bias to *doom to almost certain failure* even the best-marshalled plan to resurrect America.
5) A high probability of failure should not preclude doing what is right.

Question: How many True Americans would it take to resurrect America?

Answer: As many as are capable of making such a commitment starting with the smallest, purest, most essential and only sovereign minority that has ever existed.

The minority of one.

A Personal America

What can one True American do?

One True American can accept the responsibility of consciousness and understand what America was, in theory and for a while in reality, and then with honest and objective vision see what America has become and decide: "This stops here," which means saying *NO!* to further subjugation and acting accordingly.

What would it mean to say *NO!* and act accordingly?

It would mean drawing a line around one's free and sovereign person and never again re-drawing that line out of fear or for the sake of convenience, expediency, or comfort. It would mean being fully deliberately conscious of what defines a free human being, identifying the principles that make such freedom possible, and never again allowing those principles to be compromised, subverted, or denied. It would mean upholding and defending the supreme law of our land, the Constitution from which all other law must objectively derive.

In *Atlas Shrugged* Ayn Rand wrote:[1]

If you find a chance to vanish into some wilderness out of their reach, do so, but not to exist as a bandit or to create a gang competing with their

racket; build a productive life of your own with
those who accept your moral code and are willing to struggle for a human existence. . . .

Act as a rational being and aim at becoming a
rallying point for all those who are starved for a
voice of integrity — act on your rational values,
whether alone in the midst of your enemies, or
with a few of your chosen friends, or as the
founder of a modest community on the frontier
of mankind's rebirth.

This is the ideological answer to "What can one True
American do?" It is the answer closest to America's moral
and legal underpinnings and that forms the basis for the
practical answer, which is: learn, stand, share, act, never
compromise, be ever vigilant.

If you are still reading this book you are probably not
among what John Adams described as "multitudes of honest and well meaning though weak and mistaken people"
— which today becomes "multitudes of honest, well-
meaning, fearful, normalcy-bias-impaired, convenience-
dependent, circus-games-distracted, privacy-squandering,
weak and mistaken people waiting for someone to lead
them out of a mess deeper than they comprehend." You
are probably not among those who, when researching the
veracity of controversial information, look no further than
Wikipedia or "fact checkers" in the pay of America's enemies. You may even realize that what has so far failed to
prevent America from sinking into the grave of Fascism[2]
— which is not a late stage of dying but an early stage of
decomposition — does not now have the power to resurrect America from that grave.

Among multitudes of honest, well-meaning, fearful,
normalcy-bias-impaired, convenience-dependent, circus-

games-distracted, privacy-squandering, weak and mistaken people waiting for someone to lead them out of a
mess deeper than they comprehend, what *can* one True
American do?

One True American can learn.

"Sit down before fact as a little child," wrote Thomas
Henry Huxley,[3] "be prepared to give up every preconceived notion, follow humbly wherever and to whatever
abysses nature leads, or you shall learn nothing."

Seek information, news, and advice from sources not
beholden to outside influence — which eliminates all of
corporate media, most popular talk shows, and most alternative media. Read John Locke, Alexis de Tocqueville,
Thomas Jefferson, Isabel Paterson, Ayn Rand, Aldous
Huxley, George Orwell, Thomas Paine, and America's
Declaration of Independence and Constitution. Every pre-
cept for the intact survival of a free nation has already,
decades ago, been clearly stated, painstakingly explained,
and unassailably defended by minds more intelligent,
perceptive, and accurately predictive than today's cele-
brated pro-America personages who borrow, adapt, and
restate what has already been stated to fortify new books,
lectures, essays, and "shows."

If your approach to learning is unprejudiced you will
understand that the Republic of America is not failing, fal-
tering, or in decline, but gone. And worse than gone: *that
the idea of America has been made a lie*. You will understand
that vast numbers of Americans have been led to believe
otherwise, buoyed by the habituated expectation that they
can vote their way out of even the grave. You will understand that America cannot be voted out of the grave and
that *if* through a pristine ballot-counting process we could
reclaim what we have lost by reversing the process of loss,

it would take until approximately 2180 before we were
sufficiently unfettered to cleanly recommence the course
America's founders made possible.

You will see . . .

That even Locke, de Tocqueville, Jefferson, Paterson,
Rand, Orwell, Paine, and America's inspiring Declaration
and Constitution failed to inspire enough Americans to
see the road they were traveling and change course before
life became a function of permission, before liberty became a privilege, before happiness became a redefined, if
not impossible, dream.

That America's steady self-betrayal cannot be reversed by hoping and voting or by any method attempted
since 1776.

That America's enemies rely on a trusting, benevolent, specifically *American* outlook, tossing every now and
again a few rationed crumbs called "good news," comfort-
able in the likelihood that victims grateful for crumbs
while waiting for a leader and reconciliation are incapable
of doing what is necessary to restore the principles that
gave birth to America.

That America's enemies are impotent sans inattentive
compliance, fearful acquiescence, and cowed obedience.

That it is not enough to "question everything." That
one must *rethink* everything.

That the guard on the bridge between liberty and enslavement has always been self-respect.

One True American can stand.

In *The Shootist*,[4] author Glendon Swarthout described
the frontier philosophy of his gunslinger protagonist, John
Bernard Books: "I won't be wronged, I won't be insulted,
and I won't be laid a-hand on. I don't do these things to
other people, and I require the same from them."

Overly simple? Context limited? Perhaps, but Books' personal code is more than what most people consciously articulate for themselves, and rules consciously articulated can mean the heartbeat-spaced difference between liberty and enslavement, life and death. Contemplate, select, choose, and pronounce *your* rules — then abide by them. Before one can effectively and lastingly stand against wrong, one must first know what is right.

One True American can share.

Do not keep what you learn or where you stand a secret. If and when appropriate, certainly whenever necessary, give others a chance to see who you are and what you represent. You *may* gain friends and allies; you *will* identify enemies.

One True American can act.

Stop making it easy for wannabe dictators to dictate your life. To the extent that you depend on systems controlled by government, your life depends on government. To the extent that you free yourself from these systems, you will be free from government. In other words, build for yourself a truly independent life. You will likely be surprised, perhaps appalled and embarrassed, by the absurdities a *de*pendent life dresses in the garments of "necessary" and "normal."

If you have children in public education, remove them. *Now*. Whatever you must arrange to properly educate your children — as opposed to sacrificing them to State indoctrination — *you must arrange*. Government control of education is the most powerful and durable means of achieving a totalitarian future. Complaining at school-board meetings about curriculum, reading lists, bathroom designation, and boys swimming for the girls' team is folly in the big picture because *public education is the problem*. In a free nation, it is Public Enemy Number One.

To break from government-controlled and infra-structure-dependent systems — grid power, public water and sewer, store shelves — you must relocate as far as possible from large population centers. Buying an acre or two with a private well and room for a vegetable garden on the outskirts of a small town would be a good start. Going off-grid would be better. Grow what you eat; trade goods and services with neighbors; downsize, get out of debt, perform your own home and vehicle maintenance; invest in the Second Amendment and become proficient in the right it protects; teach self-reliance to your children *by example*; stay out of the technocrats' "cloud;" reject all "smart" and trackable devices; ditch Google, Wikipedia, YouTube, Facebook, Instagram and every other censoring, propagandizing, data-mining destroyer of privacy; utilize a Virtual Proxy Network when online; safeguard your electronic communications via secure email and data encryption; refuse every offering or imposition of AI; venture into population centers only when necessary.

Oppose with your feet the United Nations' Agendas 21 and 2030[5] — one pillar of which is to herd all of humanity into micro-homes in mega-cities while converting millions of acres of sparsely populated land into forbidden zones.

Celebrate not with fireworks the Fourth of July, but with reverent reflection, *Independence Day*. In other words, make your inner world your personal America.

And get healthy.

When John D. Rockefeller leveraged his oil empire to capture American journalism and medicine, when he combined petroleum-based pharmaceutical production with an intensive campaign to politically and legally disparage natural healing as "alternative," he created the ultimate problem-reaction-solution cycle: an ill populace driven by fear of illness to dependency on a drug-manufacturing colossus motivated not to heal, but to sell. One unintended consequence of the Covid ruse was exposure of modern medicine's incompetence and corruption: choose and act according to this evidence.

One True American can refuse to compromise.

Compromise, like sacrifice, is a word nonchalantly tossed about as if its meaning is inconsequent. But its meaning is as critically consequential as the bottomless cache of "minor" compromises that sacrificed America to an early stage of decomposition. Every compromised principle is a betrayal. Every deal between right and wrong erodes right and fortifies wrong. Every bargain with bad sucks life out of good. When one understands fundamentally what is right and what the Republic of America was founded to protect and prevent, one understands that there can be no compromise in personal or national principles, which, in the biggest picture of all, assures no bargains with evil, ever.

One True American must be vigilant.

Whether it was Thomas Jefferson, Wendell Phillips, or John Philpott Curran who originated "The price of liberty is eternal vigilance," these words, like most decrees of import, have been offhandedly mouthed so often as to achieve the banality of a politician's credo. One need only contemplate America's circus-games-distracted, hokum-hooked, ease-obsessed, take-the-good-for-granted population majority to understand that the author of this decree was not only correct, but life-and-death serious.

On an Independence Day just over two centuries ago,

John Quincy Adams eloquently stated the standard of foreign policy proper to a free nation.[6] It is no less proper to a
free person, to a moral and sovereign Minority of One.

> Wherever the standard of freedom and indepen-
> dence has been or shall be unfurled, there will
> [America's] heart, her benedictions and her
> prayers, be. But she goes not abroad in search of
> monsters to destroy. She is the well-wisher to the
> freedom and independence of all; she is the
> champion and vindicator only of her own. . . .
>   She might become the dictatress of the world;
> she would be no longer the ruler of her own
> spirit.

What can one True American gain by learning, standing, sharing, acting, refusing to compromise, and remaining ever vigilant? Aware and defensible ownership of the
sacrosanct virtue that inspired America's Declaration of
Independence, that broke the chains of tyranny, that inked
the world's first liberty-based constitution: *the rights inalienable to a naturally free and sovereign human person.*

Life, Fortune, and Sacred Honor

In "How Not to Save America" I reproached for cause thirteen popular behaviors and save-America enterprises that
haven't a sugar-cube-on-an-anthill's chance of resurrect-
ing America, and I haven't the stomach to repeat what I
said in "The Unfounding" about the frivolous, superficial,
empty-headed online garbage that occupies so much time
in the lives of so many people. But to avoid any chance of

assumption, I will repeat a few noteworthy low points.

Those who cannot eliminate online-refuse consumption from their brief time on earth comprise a ready-made collective neck. To a marginally lesser degree, the same holds true for those who vicariously experience glory through sports icons, fantasy-fiction heroics, and celebrity adoration. Those who prefer circus games and virtual associations to reality and life deserve every bad consequence their ignorance makes possible.

And those who truly believe that "pushing back" is an effective tool of self-defense — that children belong in a fight between grown-ups — that politics is the problem and that voting will produce a real and lasting American renaissance — that the cure for Leftist media is Conservative media — that Americans need sponsor-beholden talk-show personalities to pre-chew their news — that group identity has any place in a nation founded on the rights of the individual — that merging church and State constitutes a moral good — or, saving the supreme guilt for last, that those who are paid to work for a corrupt government or corporation are not *themselves* the enablers and perpetuators of corruption — may as well take their place against the wall while there's room.

If, however, you are an American in the original sense of the word, I invite you to say *NO!* to the wannabe statist controllers whose plan has long been to destroy the pro-human, pro-liberty philosophical root of the idea that made America possible, and to act accordingly. To that end I offer a Second Declaration of Independence, presented as the final chapter of this book and downloadable at TheSecondDeclaration.org.

Like its predecessor, this Declaration frames a list of unconscionable offenses imposed by a tyrannical government upon a free citizenry. Unlike its predecessor, these named grievances violate not only the natural rights that exist with or without legal recognition and protection, but the contract authored by Original Americans to enshrine and forever protect those rights.

Whether this Second Declaration serves as a personal reminder of what our government has become — or as a rallying cry for those whose rights have been stolen by an insolently anti-America government — or as a published proclamation of *NO!* to every functionary of that government — I invite you to formally identify and establish an inviolable Tyranny Barrier around your free and sovereign person, a perimeter defensible morally and by reference to America's original Constitution.

But, you might wonder, what if only one person is willing to say *NO!* and act accordingly? Or understands that Patrick Henry's liberty-and-death pronouncement was and remains more than "just words"? Or respects unconditionally the requirements of life as a sovereign human being and the incomparable worth of a republic created to protect those requirements?

What if only one person is willing to pledge Life, Fortune, and sacred Honor to a generations-overdue Second Declaration of Independence?

Well — what if?

Beyond my plan for this Second Declaration its future is out of my hands, but were I to discover that I am the only person in America for whom it has meaning?

So be it. This is simply what one True American is willing to make real.

What are you willing to make real?

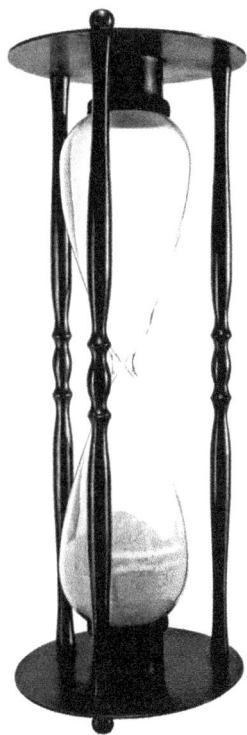

O

RESURRECTING AMERICA:
A SECOND DECLARATION
of
INDEPENDENCE

We, Sovereign Citizens of the Sovereign Nation
of America, by Right and by Declaration, do hereby pledge
to restore to its Just place in our Lives and in the
World, our Constitutional Republic.

W hen in the course of human events it becomes
necessary for a people to reclaim the righteous
political bands that once connected them with their
once-righteous government but that have, through ignorance,
neglect, and treachery, been forsaken and betrayed, and to
assume among the powers of the earth the natural and proper
relationship between individuals and peoples that the Laws of
Nature and of Nature's God entitle them, respect for humankind
requires that they should declare the causes that impel them to
proclaim their intentions.

We hold these truths to be self-evident:

That all men are created equal;

That they are endowed by their Creator with certain
inalienable Rights;

That among these are Life, Liberty and the pursuit of
Happiness;

That to secure these Rights, the Constitutional Republic of
the United States of America was instituted, wrested from
tyranny by Declaration and Blood, deriving its just power
from the consent of the governed in accordance with its
Constitution, which is the supreme Law of the Land;

That should the government of a Republic so instituted
become destructive of these ends and of the Constitution
from which it derives its limited authority, it is the Right of
the People to reclaim from this government the authority
entrusted to it by the People, and to restore to its
Constitutional origin by whatever means most justly
expedient, their Republic.

Prudence dictates that governments long established should not
be changed for light and transient causes, and experience has

shown that a people are more disposed to suffer while evils are sufferable than to right themselves by abolishing the wrongful forms to which they have become accustomed. But when a long train of abuses and usurpations, pursuing invariably the same object, evinces a design to reduce them under absolute despotism, it is their Right, it is their duty, to throw off such government and to provide new guards for their future security.

Such has been the patient sufferance of the Citizens of the Constitutional Republic of America, and such is now the necessity that constrains us to restore our founding system of government. The history of a long line of presidential, congressional, and judicial administrations is one of repeated abuses and usurpations, all having in direct object the establishment of an absolute tyranny over us. To prove this, let facts be submitted to a candid world with the understanding that we are not obliged to produce the entire cumulative America-destroying minutiae of decades, that an accurate exampling of abuses, usurpations, and un-Constitutional or anti-Constitutional Rights infringement is sufficient to warrant the demands of this document. We offer, therefore, the following in specific, if not all-inclusive, testimony.

1. The Constitution of the United States of America has been adulterated to contradict the meaning, intent, and spirit of that document as originally authored, most notoriously with Amendments XI, XIV, XVI, XVIII, and XXIII. Amendment XI enables restoration of the British common-law doctrine, rejected by America's Declaration of Independence and quashed by our Revolutionary War, that "The Sovereign" can do no wrong; Amendment XIV, through ambiguous text and undefined terms, attempts to repudiate the validity of a wronged People's Device of Last Resort, namely rebellion, properly presented in America's Declaration of Independence as a rightful necessity; Amendment XVI imposes on a productive American Citizenry a curtailment of our Right to Life, which is to say our Right to keep and use at our discretion the entirety of the result of our free productive labor; the insolently authoritarian Amendment XVIII and its unpenitent Amendment XXI repeal are sufficiently shameful as to be expunged and banished to history-footnote status; although Amendment XXII reasonably limits persons elected to the office of the President to two terms of service, Congress conspicuously failed to apply to itself an equally reasonable power constraint,

which should likewise be two terms; regarding Amendment XXIII, the District of Columbia is not a state comprised of normal American Citizens engaged in normal American life, but an abnormal aggregation of political influence and government beneficiaries — the assignment of presidential electors and quasi-state status to an unnatural, biased, corruptible social construct mocks the concept of state electors.

2. Numerous of the first ten Amendments to our Constitution, a Bill of Rights preventing government abuse of power, have been flagrantly misconstrued, abused, violated. To wit:

> Our Right to the free exercise of religion has been prohibited by the enactment of conditions upon which we may or may not exercise this Right;

> Our Right to freedom of speech has been abridged by the enactment of conditions, including censorship and speech-prohibition zones, upon which we may or may not exercise this Right;

> Our Right to freedom of the press has been abridged by the enactment of conditions — including censorship and government-designated restrictive terms such as "misinformation" and "disinformation" — upon which we may or may not exercise this Right;

> Our Right to peaceably assemble has been abridged by the enactment of conditions upon which we may or may not exercise this Right; contrarily, violent and riotous assemblies have been permitted to flourish when they advance the agenda of government administrations and/or agencies, resulting in property damage and loss of livelihoods and lives;

> Our Right to petition our government for a redress of grievances has been abridged by the enactment of conditions upon which we may or may not exercise this Right;

> Our Right to keep and bear arms has been egregiously and relentlessly infringed by administration after administration and court after court ignoring, for political gain, the incontrovertible meaning of the word "infringe;"

Our Right to be secure in our persons, houses, papers, and effects against unreasonable searches and seizures has been repeatedly and routinely violated; warrants have been issued without probable cause and by "authorities" created for the purpose of issuing otherwise-illegal warrants; property has been seized under the "authority" of similarly un-Constitutional legal inventions such as asset-forfeiture laws, under which a majority of prosecutions result in dismissals or findings of *not guilty*, often without the return of assets seized;

We have been deprived of Life, Liberty, and Property without due process of law, again under the non-authority of un-Constitutional legal inventions; private property has been taken not for public use, but for private use redefined as "beneficial to the public;"

The accused in criminal prosecutions have repeatedly and routinely been denied their Right to a speedy and public trial by an impartial jury of the state and district wherein the alleged crime was committed, and have been denied their Right to confront witnesses against them;

In suits at common law, the Right of trial by jury has been denied or judicially marginalized;

Excessive bail and fines have repeatedly and routinely been imposed; contrarily, when the actions of indicted or guilty offenders furthers the agenda of government administrations and/or agencies, bail and fines have been made perfunctory;

Rights not enumerated in the Constitution but extant in Natural Law and retained by the People, have been repeatedly and routinely disparaged and denied;

3. The present and previous presidential, congressional, and judicial administrations, hereinafter "Usurpers," have, unchecked over the course of many decades, enacted laws and regulations not only in violation of the literal meaning and legal intent of our Original Constitution, but in demonstrable harmony with the tenets of the life-destroying tyrannical regimes from which America was founded to provide safe haven.

4. Usurpers repeatedly seek to undermine States' rights and to minify under federal control by decree and fiscal bribery, that uniquely American concept.

5. Usurpers have obstructed the Administration of Justice through the creation of obscure and ambiguous laws that make us unwitting criminals for infractions of which we are, and reasonably should be, unaware.

6. Usurpers have obstructed the Administration of Justice by effecting a multi-tiered System of *Injustice*, politically biased in its interpretation, application, enforcement, and sentencing.

7. Usurpers have obstructed the Administration of Justice by staging for public show, mock trials of one type for contrived offenses by contrived offenders, and of another type for actual crimes committed by the politically connected, influential, or useful.

8. Usurpers have obstructed the Administration of Justice by politicizing not only the criminal code, but the judicial branch and its enforcement arm.

9. In contravention of America's fair and reasonable self-protective immigration laws, Usurpers have obstructed the Administration of Justice by inviting, baiting, sponsoring, and granting access to and domicile within the Republic of America, undocumented foreign nationals from countries not only incompatible with and unfriendly to the Republic of America, but openly hostile to the Republic of America. They have done so to the endangerment of border-property owners, to the detriment of border-states Citizens and those in recipient towns and cities, and to the long-term ideological and cultural impairment of the Republic of America, no doubt for that very purpose.

10. By politicizing and undermining military-enlistment standards, Usurpers have obstructed and crippled the Administration of National Self-Defense, willfully transitioning a powerful America-protecting force into a poster institution of fashionable social conscience.

11. Usurpers have personally profited from defense and weapons-manufacture contracts and foreign military intervention.

12. Usurpers have by degrees over time militarized and federalized municipal departments of law enforcement, providing combat-grade armament and encouraging a Citizens-as-suspects attitude, effectively creating domestic standing armies within a federal police state.

13. Usurpers have criminally undertaken, and covertly expanded to offshore facilities, the manufacture of biological- and chemical-warfare materiel.

14. Usurpers have crafted for themselves a semi-permanent ruling class while perfecting the duplicitous practice of amassing personal wealth by means of political position and legalized confiscation. Our government employees have bastardized American government for the purpose of anointing themselves our moneyed masters.

15. Usurpers have criminally used their positions of elected and appointed authority as levers for familial enrichment by trading political influence with corporations and foreign governments.

16. Usurpers have, through regulatory machination and by means of loans, payments, and grants coercively taken from us via taxation, annexed and politicized the fields of science, education, energy production, communication, and medicine; they have further hijacked a multitude of commercial enterprises including air and rail travel, automobile design, and household-product manufacture.

17. Usurpers have transferred to foreign governments, including to hostile foreign governments, by means of deed, promise, or as instruments of debt, tracts of sovereign-America real estate, and have allowed foreign governments to seize assets, improvements, and equipment — from the Panama Canal to oil-field infrastructure to military weaponry — belonging by Right to American Citizens.

18. Usurpers have in spirit, if not yet fully in law, condemned under the classification "domestic terrorist" all manner of dissenting opinion and expectation of grievance redress communicated by American Citizens, when in reality it is the Usurpers who are, by word and deed, propagating terror throughout domestic America.

19. Usurpers have conspired with foreign governments and entities for the purpose of making Sovereign America subservient to globalist conglomerates such as the United Nations and World Health Organization.

20. Usurpers have imposed every conceivable manner of onerous taxation upon us.

21. Usurpers have openly undertaken to wage war against us by means of police and federal-agency raids on private property, not for the purpose of dangerous-criminal apprehension, but for the purpose of inflicting fear and terror among the Citizenry.

22. Usurpers have, by means of subterfuge, attempted to provoke and successfully provoked American Citizens to engage in illegal acts of a political and violent nature, thereby furthering the goals of the administration and/or agencies involved, including plots to kidnap a state governor and to stage an "insurrection" on U.S. Capital grounds.

23. Usurpers have encouraged and/or failed to prevent criminally violent riots resulting in property destruction, theft, trauma, injury, and death.

24. Usurpers have created an immense network of federal departments, offices, and agencies unaccountable to the American Citizenry and indefensibly wasteful of monies expropriated via taxation. They have dispatched into the American Citizenry legions of officers and agents to harass and bully said Citizenry, permitting these departments, offices, and agencies to subjectively interpret existing law while creating and enforcing regulations that trespass upon and un-Constitutionally violate the Rights and private lives of American Citizens. These offices and agencies include, but are not limited to:

> Central Intelligence Agency; Federal Bureau of Investigation; Internal Revenue Service; Department of Homeland Security; Department of Education; Bureau of Educational and Cultural Affairs; Food and Drug Administration; U.S. Department of Agriculture; Federal Communications Commission; Interstate Commerce Commission; Securities and Exchange Commission; Federal Trade Commission; Social Security Administration; Selective Service System; Federal Emergency Management Agency; Bureau of Alcohol, Tobacco, Firearms and Explosives; Environmental Protection Agency; Federal National Mortgage Association; Federal Home Loan Mortgage Corporation; Federal Housing Finance Agency; Federal Housing Administration; Office of Fair Housing and Equal Opportunity; Financial Industry Regulatory Authority; Farm Credit

Administration; Commission of Fine Arts; National Endowment for the Arts; National Endowment for the Humanities; Small Business Administration; Office of Small and Disadvantaged Business Utilization; Bureau of Economic and Business Affairs; Bureau of Democracy, Human Rights, and Labor; Consumer Product Safety Commission; Equal Employment Opportunity Commission; Employee Benefits Security Administration; Office of Labor-Management Standards; National Council on Disability; Office of the Chief Economist; Office of Community Planning and Development; National Science Board; Occupational Safety and Health Administration; Office of Drug and Alcohol Policy and Compliance; National Labor Relations Board; Federal Labor Relations Authority; Privacy and Civil Liberties Oversight Board; Election Assistance Commission; Federal Election Commission; Corporation for Public Broadcasting; Women's Bureau; U.S. Agency for Global Media; U.S. Commission for the Preservation of America's Heritage Abroad; U.S. Commission on International Religious Freedom; National Indian Gaming Commission; Bureau of Medical Services; Bureau of Global Talent Management; Office of the U.S. Global AIDS Coordinator and Health Diplomacy; Office of the Special Inspector General for Pandemic Recovery; Canine and Equine Governance Board; Office of Biometric Identity Management; Office of the Chief Human Capital Officer; 113 offices, administrations, institutes, and agencies of the U.S. Department of Health and Human Services; every facet of the Federal Reserve System.

25. Usurpers have established a system of rules, regulations, permissions, and operational controls over private American businesses in full concordance with the tenets of Fascism.

26. Usurpers have ordained themselves the ultimate arbiters of business necessity, success, and failure; they have imposed and prosecuted pronouncements of "essential" and "nonessential;" they have expropriated massive sums of money from us for the purpose of rescuing from failure select corporations Usurpers deem exempt from the rules of sound business management and market demand.

27. Usurpers have recklessly and with increasing intensity, primarily but not exclusively by means of a private-banking cartel disingenuously called the Federal Reserve and by out-of-thin-air printing of money backed only by the promise of future tax collection, devalued our currency by almost 100 percent in approximately as many years. We have, accordingly, been deprived of legitimate currency with tangible value, and we have been made responsible for a national debt so immense as to be, if not forfeited in bankruptcy, the responsibility of untold indentured generations of unborn Americans.

28. Usurpers have immorally and illegally "democratically" forced us to become participants in a "Social Security" scheme that deprives us of our Right to manage our private financial

affairs, including our savings and investments, by coercively transferring our wealth to government.

29. Usurpers have, in a barefaced manifestation of Socialism via the un-Constitutional Patient Protection and Affordable Care Act buttressed by a Constitution-defying Supreme Court, forcibly corralled Americans into a government healthcare scheme.

30. Usurpers have stolen America's future by transforming an already-Rights-violating prescribed-by-law government-controlled educational system into a national collectivist program of child indoctrination.

31. Usurpers have, for the purpose of coercively financing the aforementioned program of child indoctrination, made conditional upon payment of "property tax" our Right to own the land and improvements that are the earthly foundation on which we enjoy Life and Liberty and from which we pursue Happiness. By any honest definition of ownership, such an extortion makes every property titleholder a mere tenant at the mercy of a government landlord, subject to eviction for nonpayment of "rent" and stripping us of the Right that makes every other Right actionable, effectively nullifying Constitutional Amendment IV and making each of us the sponsor of a stolen American future.

32. Usurpers have led Americans to fight, suffer, and die in foreign lands by means of deception, including self-inflicted wounds and fabricated intelligence such as the Vietnam War's Gulf of Tonkin incident and the Gulf War's "weapons of mass destruction" lie. As evidence continues to be gathered by stalwart seekers of justice, and despite suppression by propagandist media, the attacks of 11 September 2001 and the alleged pandemic of 2020 appear more and more to qualify as government-complicit false-flag events.

33. Usurpers have, through the enactment of calamitous domestic policies, caused numerous of our cities to deteriorate into minor war zones, rife with unprevented open violence. Criminal offenders, if apprehended, are unpunished or insufficiently punished and released back into a society in which they are unable to function peacefully. Streets, sidewalks, and parks have become refugee camps strewn with bodies, trash, drug paraphernalia, and excrement, resembling more closely a return

to the Dark Ages than civilized modernity. And while criminals do what criminals do without fear of just government reprisal, honest Citizens live in fear of an unjust government.

34. Usurpers have established throughout the land a condition of presumed guilt under which all Citizens are treated like criminal suspects. By means of constant intrusive monitoring, surveillance, body scans, pat-downs, strip-searches, and cavity probes, increasingly without court-issued warrants or probable cause of having committed dangerous crimes, and with the enactment of regulations and laws that criminalize all manner of victimless behavior, we have been relegated to a "guilty until proven otherwise" status.

35. Usurpers have exploited to their advantage every tragedy, disaster, and threat of disaster — whether natural, man-made, or self-created — for the purpose of controlling the private lives of American Citizens under the facade of "public safety" and/or "national security," abridging at every opportunity our Constitution-protected Rights while expanding the mass, grasp, and despotic power of government, when it is during times of tragedy, disaster, and threat of disaster that our Constitution's clear limitations on government power are most urgently needed. Usurpers have, through passage of bills such as the Patriot Act, which effectively makes every American Citizen a potential threat to "national security," and the National Defense Authorization Act, which provides for Constitution-prohibited terms of Citizen detainment, sanctioned and normalized all manner of un-Constitutional conduct.

36. Usurpers have crafted and manipulated loopholes in law by redefining and subjectively construing both legal terminology and the English language for the purpose of "making legal" their Constitution-prohibited agenda. They have through such craft manufactured politically useful interpretations of words such as freedom and rights, republic and democracy, voluntary and mandatory, self-defense, due process, terrorist, extremist, insurrection, pandemic, vaccine, and life, sowing confusion, embedding intimidation, and inflicting all manner of harm upon the American Citizenry. Usurpers systematically ignore and excoriate the fact that words have definitions apart from what Usurpers *want* words to mean, including simple biological

nomenclature and Constitutional designation.

37. Usurpers have constructed, officially encouraged, and politicized a culture of inversion, both moral and literal. Rogue disingenuous government operatives routinely blame honest Americans of endorsing, doing, and undertaking to do the very wrongs they themselves endorse, do, and undertake to do — a key trait of pathological liars. Usurpers routinely elevate to political preeminence choices and behaviors that are, as they should be, the exclusive concern of the private parties involved.

38. Usurpers have, through the aforementioned Constitution-defying departments, offices, and agencies, harassed, intimidated, threatened, injured, and murdered American Citizens whose affiliations, opinions, occupations, and lifestyle choices are perceived as threats to Usurpers and their goals.

39. Usurpers have for decades criminally subjected American Citizens, without their consent and through stealth, secrecy, manipulation, and deceit, to all manner of bodily and psychological harm. From Operation Mockingbird and MK Ultra to crippling and lethal "medical" experimentation performed on orphaned children, Southern blacks, and soldiers — from encircling the globe with untested 5G radiation to, while denying that the technology exists, blanketing our skies with jet-dispersed aerosolized metals — from making corporate media their Department of Propaganda to circumventing Constitution-prohibited censorship by suborning or partnering with "private" forums for public expression — from proscribing proven medications to mandating as "safe and effective" an inadequately tested gene-altering experimental injection, which time and evidence have overwhelmingly shown to be neither safe nor effective, allegedly for the purpose of preventing transmission of an alleged novel, negligibly lethal "flu-like" virus.

40. Usurpers have created for themselves a system wherein personal liability is divorced from government-functionary wrongdoing unless such liability serves a political agenda. Ranging from elected and appointed officials lying to us and to Congress, to agency and law officers committing un-onstitutional acts and violence against innocents, government functionaries have been exempted, actually pre-exonerated, *by government* from

the punishment to which we Citizens would be aggressively subjected, and costs associated with government-functionary wrongdoing, including civil-lawsuit settlement, are assigned to us in the form of taxation.

41. Usurpers have captured and corrupted America's election process by imposing a manipulable two-party construct of syndicate-approved and syndicate-chosen candidates, and by comprehensively deploying a vote-tabulation infrastructure susceptible to interference, tampering, falsification, and contamination by malevolent local, state, national, and foreign actors.

42. Usurpers have elevated to the status of Monarchical Decree the promiscuous issuance of Executive Orders.

43. America's judicial system, intended to be a fortress of Constitutional preservation and defense, has become handmaiden to and enabler of the Usurpers, whether fouled by ignorance, personal political activism, Constitution illiteracy, bribery, or blackmail is irrelevant. With increasingly rare exceptions, jurists into whose hands the People have entrusted Constitutional Law are not dealing Constitutional Law. Their hands are withered, corrupted, made for show, dead.

44. _____

In summary, almost the entire system of America's government — from town councils to the U.S. Capital and White House, from municipal courts to the Supreme Court — has become a multi-headed Tyrant and American Citizens have been made a population of subjects. What was established and guaranteed by Constitutional Contract to be the protector of inalienable Rights has become the established violator of these Rights. The government of the United States of America, with the passive sanction of, as John Adams opined in 1776, "multitudes of honest and well meaning though weak and mistaken people," stands in flagrant breach of its Constitutional Contract.

Throughout the evolution and expansion of these transgressions we have petitioned for redress in the most earnest terms across a span of decades — in public meetings, in letters to our elected representatives, via on-air and online discussions and announcements. Our petitions have been misrepresented by a government-controlled corporate media and answered by false promises and repeated injury. The entrenched and now-historical presidential, congressional, and judicial administrations responsible for such longstanding un-Constitutional offenses define, in their composite, the character of a Tyrant deaf to the voice of justice and of consanguinity and unfit to govern in any capacity a free People.

Two and a half centuries ago, to a lesser registry of grievances, America's Declaration of Independence pronounced in conclusion:

> We, therefore, the Representatives of the United States of America, in General Congress, Assembled, appealing to the Supreme Judge of the world for the rectitude of our intentions, do, in the Name, and by Authority of the good People of these Colonies, solemnly publish and declare, That these United Colonies are, and of Right ought to be Free and Independent States; that they are Absolved from all Allegiance to the British Crown, and that all political connection between them and the State of Great Britain, is and ought to be totally dissolved; and that as Free and Independent States, they have full Power to levy War, conclude Peace, contract Alliances, establish Commerce, and to do all other Acts and Things which Independent States may of right do. And for the support of this Declaration, with a firm reliance on the protection of divine Providence, we mutually pledge to each other our Lives, our Fortunes and our sacred Honor.

The British Crown's refusal to recognize American colonists' Rights as a free and sovereign People necessitated the penning of that Declaration. Although the resulting violent conflict has been called a revolution, a rebellion, and an insurrection, it was in truth none of these for a single reason:

> *The natural and just relationship between individuals and peoples and their representatives in government is one of inviolable respect for the inalienable Rights of every person.*

The bold and certain assertion of these Rights is, therefore,
the requisite maintenance of a natural and just relationship.
Those who would use force to usurp these Rights or
extinguish this relationship under Color of Law are
themselves the seditious initiates of revolution, rebellion, and
insurrection against a natural and just relationship.

Whereas the British Crown treated colonial-America Citizens in a manner suited to and supportive of a monarchical Tyrant, the government of America has for decades and with increasing fervor treated American Citizens in a manner unsuited to and destructive of a free Constitutional Republic. And whereas the Government of America was founded to be the Protector of the inalienable Rights of Americans — of Life, Liberty, and the pursuit of Happiness — it has become the controller and dispenser of these Rights as if Rights are privileges. It has become, in a thousand ways and under Color of Law, the very Tyrant America was founded to eternally forfend.

We, Sovereign Citizens of the Constitutional Republic of America, are not obliged to re-declare to our government what America's founders' declared to the British Crown. That glorious Declaration was lucidly and responsibly published and the Constitutional document that was its result is likewise already in existence. Furthermore, this Constitutional document:

Does not have an expiration date;

Is not conditional upon majority vote, approval, or conformation;

Is written in plain English unresponsive to subjective interpretation by latter-day legal scholars, agency bureaucrats, self-serving politicians, or politicized judges;

Is morally and legally impervious to breach by those whose low character and corrupt goals are threatened by its existence.

This Second Declaration of American Independence is a categorical affirmation of what exists and from whence the allegiance of True Americans originates. We who understand that inalienable Rights are absolute Rights — who recognize that the purpose of our Original Constitution was and remains the protection of individual Americans from tyranny in all its forms, including the Tyranny of the Majority, commonly known as "democracy" — herein assert that our Original Constitution is the supreme Law of *our* Land, that we abide by this Law and expect without exception that our employees in government abide by this Law. We further recognize and herein assert that Citizens who renounce this founding and defining document are, by choice, not Americans, and that elected and appointed officials who disregard or betray what they have sworn to uphold are traitors to their oath and to the Republic of America.

We will not be intimidated by, nor yield to, the tyrannical functionaries of a Constitution-defiling government, and we ask of our fellow Citizens:

> That those who are Americans in the Original Constitutional sense follow our example by refusing to acquiesce to the dictates of a government we have allowed to become a Tyrant, and that those who renounce America's founding and defining document hold themselves to an honorable standard by emigrating to a nation ruled by the democratic despotism they clearly prefer to a liberty-protecting Constitutional Republic.

Of our employees in government we require:

> That you whose solemn work it is to enforce America's laws understand that we are innocent Citizens, not guilty-until-proven-otherwise suspects, and that the sole reason for the existence of your positions is to protect the American Citizenry from force and fraud within the clear parameters established by our Constitution. And we demand, as is our Right to demand, that you hold yourselves to an honorable standard by staying true to your oath to defend our Republic's Constitution against all enemies, including if necessary against your superior officers. *In the absence of honorable standards, you may regard this Declaration as our recognition of your choice to act as enemies of America's Constitution, of the Republic of America, and of Americans.*

> That you whose solemn work it is to militarily defend the Republic of America from foreign aggression hold yourselves to an honorable standard by staying true to your

oath to defend our Republic's Constitution and Citizenry against all enemies, including if necessary against your superior officers and Commander in Chief. *In the absence of honorable standards, you may regard this Declaration as our recognition of your choice to act as enemies of America's Constitution, of the Republic of America, and of Americans.*

That you whose solemn work it is to adjudicate American law, whose responsibility to our Constitution is of greatest effect, hold yourselves to an honorable standard by staying true to your oath to defend our Republic's Constitution against all enemies, including if necessary against members of the legislative and executive branches, government-department functionaries, and personal political inclination. *In the absence of honorable standards, you may regard this Declaration as our recognition of your choice to act as enemies of America's Constitution, of the Republic of America, and of Americans.* In such an absence you will be, and we will so charge you:

In Contempt of the Constitution
of the United States of America.

In conclusion, appealing to the highest moral authority for the rectitude of our intentions and disdaining elected representatives complicit in America's ruin, we, Sovereign Citizens of the Sovereign Republic of America, do solemnly declare:

That we are free individuals with inalienable Rights forever secured by America's Original Constitution;

That our failure to discern and prevent the erosion of our Rights and our willingness to suffer evils to which we became accustomed, do not constitute a forfeiture or a diminishing of our Rights;

That our government has for many decades, by means of incremental abuses and usurpations, pursued as its object the establishment of absolute tyranny over us;

That we do not recognize any authority claimed by our government to direct our lives as if we were its subjects;

That all political connections between us and every

Constitutional-contract-breaching governing body in America is, in consequence of said breach, dissolved in principle, in fact, and in law to immediate effect.

We, therefore, as witnesses to and victims of the nefarious plundering of our inalienable Rights, declare the present government of America to be the Enemy of Americans. We declare that we will not countenance this ignoble condition by continuing to acquiesce to the Constitution-betraying, liberty-debasing, treasonous dictates of its miscreant functionaries. We further declare that we will, by our actions as Sovereign persons and as is our Right, restore to its Just place in our Lives and in the World what Tyrants at every level of government have ravaged unto extinction:

The Constitutional Republic of America.

For the support of this Declaration, with a firm reliance on the founding and defining principles of the Constitutional Republic of America, we solemnly pledge our Lives, our Fortunes, and our sacred Honor.

AFTERWORD

The power of normalcy bias is such that even first-hand-witnessed bias-dispelling evidence can fail to break its comforting spell. When substantially shaken it tends not to retreat like an upright adversary, but to claw and cling and rationalize like a caught-in-the-act abuser wanting a second chance.

Although I had since the early 1980s been aware of America's incremental self-betrayal, it was not until the late 1990s that I recognized my government's capacity not merely for criminal negligence, but for willful evil, and it was not until the summer of 2014 that I recognized this capacity as standard operating procedure. Upon learning that an American-intelligence asset had murdered the owner of the lovely Guatemala-farm hostelry where I was a guest (see *Once Upon a Time on a Bicycle*), my inquiries led me to Jennifer K. Harbury's 2005 exposé, *Truth, Torture, and the American Way* — and then to the work of journalists investigating America's participation in rights violations in other countries — and then back to, with opened eyes, my government's crimes against American citizens.

A longtime friend, a world-champion American athlete and somewhat cynical world traveler, once told me that I was, despite having experienced a uniquely adventurous life, the most un-streetwise person she had ever met. It would take the murder of a man I never knew and a lie told by someone I thought I knew before I owned the meaning of my friend's observation.

I never assumed *good* to be universal but I failed to see the danger in projecting personal inner-world benevolent values to an outer world rife with wannabe controllers. Since I could not imagine wanting to control the life of another person (or a million other persons), I could not credit as real such a pathetic other-dependent ambition. This failure of imagination may of itself not be weakness, but it is a sustainer of normalcy bias and a life-threatening vulnerability unless expanded by either the trauma of personal experience or an objective evidence-respecting tour through the darker world behind the dark world of wannabe controllers.

I recommend the tour.

Regarding where to find guides who shine light into this darkness, they will not be best-selling authors or Fox News guests or FCC-tethered show hosts, but brave souls disparaged or ignored by the mainstream and discredited by "fact-checkers." The closer independent thinkers come to exposing government-hidden truth, the harder they will be to find.

But they are worth finding.

To those willing to make the effort I sincerely wish — "whether alone in the midst of your enemies, or with a few of your chosen friends, or as the founder of a modest community on the frontier of mankind's rebirth" — a free, productive, happy life in *your own personal America.*

Michael Russell

NOTES

Citations preceded by an asterisk are of singular importance.

10 | America and the Law of Identity

9 | Taking Justice Back from Dead Hands: A Premise

1   Hill, Napoleon, *Think and Grow Rich* (1937) (The Ralston Society, 1948).
2   Christensen, Josh, "Soros Prosecutors Run Half of America's Largest Jurisdictions" (freebeacon.com, Jun 2022);
    Thayer, Parker, "Living Room Pundit's Guide to Soros District Attorneys" (Capital Research Center, Jan 2022).
3   Wister, Owen, *The Virginian* (The MacMillan Company, 1902).

8 | Public Enemy #2: Normalcy Bias

1   Hitler, Adolf, *Mein Kampf* (Franz Eher Verlag, 1925).
2   Chang, Iris, *The Rape of Nanking* (Basic Books, 1997).
3   *Paterson, Isabel, *The God of the Machine* (1943) (The Caxton Printers, 1968).
4   Juvenal (Decimus Iunius Iuvenalis), *Satire X* (ca 120 A.D.).
5   *Webb, Whitney, *One Nation Under Blackmail* (Trine Day, 2022).
6   *See research by Thomas Cowen, Andrew Kaufman, Michael Yeadon, Sally Fallon Morrell, David Icke, Sam Bailey, Reiner Fuëllmich, Jon Rapaport, Karen Kingston, Wolfgang Wodarg.
7   Filip, Birsen, "The WHO's Pandemic Treaty: The End of National Sovereignty and Freedom" (Mises Institute, Jun 2022);
    Knightly, Kit, "'Pandemic Treaty' Will Hand WHO Keys to Global Government" (off-guardian.org, Apr 2022).

7 | Public Enemy #1: Public Education

1   Russell, Michael, *Honor Student*, 2nd Ed. (Nonesmanneslond, 2019).
2   Menken, H.L., *The American Mercury*, Apr 1924.
3   *Schuman, Tomas, "Love Letter to America" (Almanac Panorama, 1984).

6 | Censorship's Swindling Cousin and the Simplest Word in the World

1   McWhorter, John, "The Dictionary Definition of Racism Has to Change" (*The Atlantic*, Jun 2020).
2   *Orwell, George, *Nineteen Eighty-Four* (Harcourt, Brace and Company, 1949).

5 | Censorship's Swindling Cousin and the Murder of Meaning

1   *Gentleman's Agreement* (Twentieth Century Fox, 1947).
2   Kamm, Oliver, *Accidence Will Happen: The Non-Pedantic Guide to the English Language* (W&N, 2015).

4 | How Not to Save America

1 *The Rifleman*, "Sharpshooters" (Four Star - Zane Grey, 1958).
2 *Mandate for Leadership 2025* (heritage.org, 2023).
3 Rand, Ayn, *Anthem* (Cassell, 1938).
4 Collins, Suzanne, *The Hunger Games* (Scholastic Press, 2008).
5 Wong, Julia Carrie, "Former Facebook Executive: Social Media is Ripping Society Apart" (*The Guardian*, Dec 2017);
   Lewis, Paul, "Our Minds Can be Hijacked" (*The Guardian*, Oct 2017).
6 Schuman, "Love Letter to America."

3 | Taking Justice Back from Dead Hands: A Reckoning

1 *Webster, Daniel, "On Conscription," Dec 1814 (constitution.org).
2 Waxman, Matthew, "Remembering the Selective Draft Law Cases" (lawfaremedia.org, Jan 2022);
   "Selective Draft Law Cases" (casetext.com).
3 Joondeph, Brian C., "The Incredible Vanishing Flu" (*American Thinker*, Jul 2021).
4 *Omicron* (Lux Compagnie Cinématographique de France, 1963).

2 | The Unfounding

1 Adams, John, "Letter from John Adams to Abigail Adams," 3 Jul 1776 (Massachusetts Historical Society, masshist.org).
2 Paterson, *The God of the Machine*.
3 Ibid.
4 *Griffin, G. Edward, *The Creature from Jekyll Island* (American Media, 1994).
5 *Russo, Aaron, *America – Freedom to Fascism*, 2005 (archive.org).
6 Falcon, Billy, "Sleeping Giant" (*Never Surrender*, billyfalcon.com, 2022).
7 Paterson, *The God of the Machine*.
8 Franklin, Benjamin, "Letter to Jean-Baptiste Le Roy," Nov 1789.
9 Paterson, *The God of the Machine*.
10 *Rand, Ayn, "Don't Let it Go" (1971), *Philosophy: Who Needs It* (Bobbs Merrill, 1982).
11 Ibid.
12 McCarthy, Cormac, *No Country for Old Men* (Alfred A. Knopf, 2005).
13 *Judgment at Nuremberg* (Metro-Goldwyn-Mayer Studios, 1961).
14 *Bamford, James, *Body of Secrets* (Doubleday, 2001).
15 *Prouty, L. Fletcher, *JFK: The CIA, Vietnam and the Plot to Assassinate John F. Kennedy* (Skyhorse, 2011).
16 Cohen, Jeff, and Norman, Solomon, "30-Year Anniversary: Tonkin Gulf Lie Launched Vietnam War" (fair.org, Jul 1994).
17 Wagner, Brecken A., and Lynch, Blake, E., "The Incident at Ruby Ridge" (seoklaw.com, Apr 2015).
18 *Waco: The Rules of Engagement* (Journeyman Pictures, 1997).
19 *Icke, David, *The Trigger* (Ickonic Publishing, 2019).
20 Ibid.

21 *Robinson, Mindy, *Route 91: Uncovering the Cover-Up*, 2022 (bitchute.com).

22 Baker, Steve, "What I Saw on January 6th in Washington, DC" (thepragmaticconstitutionalist.locals.com, Apr 2023).

23 Paterson, *The God of the Machine*.

24 Rand, "Don't Let it Go."

25 Carlson, Tucker, "Cling to Your Taboos" (Tucker on Twitter, Jun 2023).

26 Durden, Tyler, "'Trust Your Gut': Tucker Carlson Warns of Chaos, Ignoring Your Instincts During 'History-Changing' Events" (*Zero Hedge*, Nov 2023).

27 Worthington, Amy, "Chemtrails: Aerosol and Electromagnetic Weapons in the Age of Nuclear War" (globalresearch.ca, Dec 2017);

Tang, Aaron with Kemp, Luke, "A Fate Worse Than Warming? Stratospheric Aerosol Injection and Global Catastrophic Risk" (Frontiers in Climate, frontiersin.com, Nov 2021);

Wigington, Dane (geoengineeringwatch.org);

Feney, Sam, "Chemtrails are not a theory, they are a conspiracy fact" (davidicke.com, May 2023).

28 Paterson, *The God of the Machine*.

29 Paul, Ron, "A New Year's Resolution Worth Keeping" (Ron Paul Institute, ronpaulinstitute.org, Jan 2024).

1 | What Can One True American Do?

1 Rand, "Don't Let it Go."

2 *Peikoff, Leonard, *The Ominous Parallels* (Stein and Day, 1982).

3 Huxley, Thomas Henry, "Letter to Charles Kingsley," Sep 1860.

4 Swarthout, Glendon, *The Shootist* (Doubleday, 1975).

5 Johnson, Ileana, "U.N. Agenda 21/2030 in Full Operational Mode" (thebullelephant.com, Dec 2023); "Globalism Through U.N.'s Agenda 21, Agenda 2030, and Vision 2050" (Canada Free Press, Jul 2016);

Herscu, Shoshi, *Mass Awakening* (Balboa Press, 2018);

Icke, David, "The Long Planned Agenda to Enslave Humanity" (davidicke.com, Feb 2021);

Thorner, Nancy J., "It's 1992 All Over Again: Agenda 2030 Threatens Our Way of Life" (Heartland Institute, heartland.org, Oct. 2015);

Taylor, Ron, *Agenda 21: An Expose of the United Nations' Sustainable Development Initiative and the Forfeiture of American Sovereignty and Liberties* (Taylor/Kindle Edition, 2010).

6 Adams, John Quincy, "Speech to the U.S. House of Representatives on Foreign Policy," 4 Jul 1821 (millercenter.org).

0 | A Second Declaration of Independence

Many entries are starting points for inquiry likely to be search-engine detoured to normalcy-bias-supporting media, "fact-checkers," Wikipedia, government agencies, and taxpayer-funded corporations, universities, hospitals, think tanks, foundations. Referral to a source for specific information does not imply endorsement of that source for its treatment of other information.

INDEX

H·O·N·O·R STUDENT

hon·or stu·dent [n., obs] one who successfully resists an educational system's effort to eradicate independent thought; SEE TROUBLEMAKER, REBEL, UNPERSON, OUTLAW

A NOVEL

Michael Russell

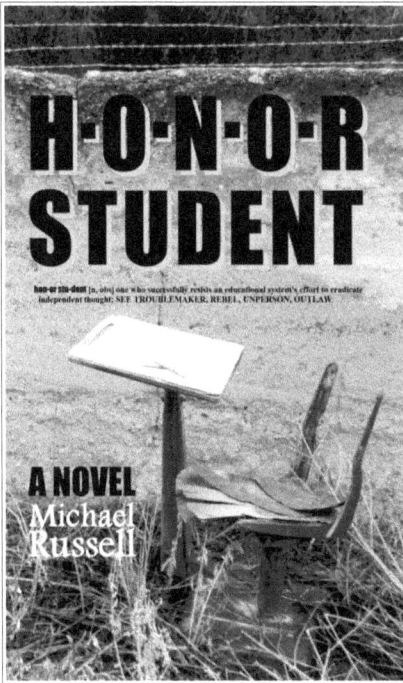

At a typical public high school in an average American city, a student is asking questions his teachers cannot answer. To his guidance counselor, his behavior is inexplicable and unnerving. To his father, school principal, he is an embarrassment. To the system, he is a threat. Kevin Saunders should be a straight-A student, yet he is failing his easiest classes as if by design.

America's founders knew the relationship between an educated citizenry and the sustaining of a free nation, but America's enemies saw opportunity in the inverse and implemented precepts designed to achieve anti-liberty ends. We are today witnessing the denouément of their campaign in the form of a citizenry needing, even longing, to be leashed and commanded.

Honor Student tells the story of a young man's fight for ownership of his mind and of an ex-teacher's struggle against self-betrayal. Its theme, the role of reason in education, is offered to anyone who has ever attended government-run Institutions for Conceptual Pacification — commonly known as public schools — but particularly to those whose minds may yet survive indoctrination.

About the Author

Michael Russell was inspired by an exuberant mentor in high school to pursue writing and teaching as a dual career, but uninspiring university classes were interrupted by a higher calling. His passion for creative mind-body integration led in his youth to professional freestyle skiing, where he won three world cups in the ballet event, and then to merging sport and art in the founding of SnowDance, a first-of-its-kind theatrical dance company on skis. With a life-long dedication to achieving excellence in every quest he has been a business manager, photographer, U.S. Freestyle Ski Team captain, logger, musician, stage actor, bartender, teacher, mechanic, motorcoach operator, inventor, builder, and, throughout, an unwavering advocate for individual rights.

He wrote the young-adult novel *Honor Student* in 1989 and a second edition thirty years later, *Once Upon a Time on a Bicycle* in 2018, *Winterdanse: The Misplaced Art of Snow Ballet* in 2022 (recipient of the International Skiing History Association's Ullr Book Award), and *The Unfounding of America* in 2024. He resides off-grid in a secluded mountain valley with his wife, German shepherds, and wild-animal neighbors. He is not on social media.

We let it happen.
We did not have to.

We were given everything
we needed to forever preserve
a haven for life and liberty:
human law, wise warnings,
eyes to see, minds to understand.
And yet we subverted the law,
ignored the warnings,
closed our eyes,
and betrayed our minds.

Our haven is gone. With it went the world.

Celandine Perreaux
Nonexistent Verse by a Nonessential Person
FEMA Sector Kansas, 2057

www.ingramcontent.com/pod-product-compliance
Lightning Source LLC
Chambersburg PA
CBHW051255020426
42333CB00025B/3215